PROGRAM
EVALUATION
IN PRACTICE

PROGRAM EVALUATION IN PRACTICE

Core Concepts and Examples for Discussion and Analysis

DEAN T. SPAULDING

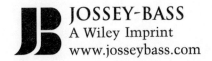

JOSSEY-BASS
A Wiley Imprint
www.josseybass.com

MT

Published by Jossey-Bass
A Wiley Imprint
989 Market Street, San Francisco, CA 94103-1741—www.josseybass.com

Jossey-Bass books and products are available through most bookstores. To contact Jossey-Bass directly call our Customer Care Department within the U.S. at 800-956-7739, outside the U.S. at 317-572-3986, or fax 317-572-4002.

Jossey-Bass also publishes its books in a variety of electronic formats. Some content that appears in print may not be available in electronic books.

Library of Congress Cataloging-in-Publication Data
Spaulding, Dean T.
  Program evaluation in practice : core concepts and examples for discussion and analysis / Dean T. Spaulding.
    p. cm.
  Includes bibliographical references and index.
  ISBN 978-0-7879-8685-8 (pbk.)
1. Educational evaluation. 2. School improvement programs—Evaluation. I. Title.
  LB2822.75.S69 2008
  379.1'58—dc22

                                                      2007041053

Printed in the United States of America

FIRST EDITION
PB Printing   10 9 8 7 6 5 4 3 2 1

5/12/08

CONTENTS

PART ONE: Introduction

PART TWO: Case Studies

LIST OF TABLES, FIGURES, AND EXHIBITS

TABLES

FIGURES

EXHIBITS

PREFACE

For over twenty years, research and literature in the area of teaching program evaluation has noted that real-world opportunities and the skills developed from such experiences are critical to the development of highly trained, highly skilled practitioners in the field of program evaluation (Brown, 1985; Chelimsky, 1997; Trevisan, 2002; Weeks, 1982). According to Trevisan and others, traditional courses in program evaluation have been designed to provide students with authentic experiences through in-course or out-of-course projects. Although both approaches have notable benefits, they are not without their share of limitations.

Didactic learning environments that utilize in-course projects have often been criticized for being too structured in their delivery. Trevisan and others note that these activities typically do not require students to leave campus or collect any "real" data that will be used by clients, in any meaningful way, to make decisions or to effect change. In such cases, these activities may consist of presenting students with a fictitious evaluation project to be designed based on a given set of goals, objectives, or variables for a fictitious agency, group, or company. Such involvement, however, typically offers no more than a cookie-cutter approach, with little room for student exploration, questioning, or growth in any sort of political or social context.

In an attempt to shift this paradigm, Trevisan (2002) describes a popular model employed by many institutions of higher education, whereby an evaluation center is established to provide a more coordinated effort toward providing an in-depth learning opportunity for evaluators-in-training. Typically these centers act as a sort of agency or consultancy and are charged with contracting with outside agencies, schools, or groups and serving as an external evaluator. According to Trevisan, this approach incorporates long-term projects of a year or more to be conducted by full-time graduate students under the direct supervision of a full-time faculty member. Trevisan notes one of the benefits of such an approach: it provides graduate students interested in the field of evaluation with long-term, realistic projects that tend to reflect much of the work, dilemmas, issues, and ethical considerations that they as professional evaluators will encounter on a daily basis.

Although this approach certainly produces an experience that is more realistic, it also presents many challenges. For example, one barrier that many instructors face when attempting to implement a more hands-on, real-world project to teach program evaluation is the infrastructural challenges of an academic setting. This infrastructure not only is challenging to faculty but also is often counterproductive and intrusive to the students' overall learning experience. For example, most institutions of higher education function within a fifteen-week semester schedule, starting in September and ending in May. Although there are certainly examples of real-world program evaluation projects that can be conducted from start to finish in such a short time (Spaulding & Lodico, 2003), the majority of real-world projects—especially those funded at the state or federal levels—have timelines that stretch out across multiple years and require annual reporting. In addition, many of these state and federal evaluation projects follow a July 1 to June 30 or August 1 to July 31 funding cycle, with the majority of data analysis and report writing necessarily occurring during the summer, when many faculty (and students) are not usually on campus.

Another barrier to teaching program evaluation with a real-world project is the variability in the quality of the experiences from project to project. One difficulty with using real-world projects is that they are out of the hands of the instructor. In some cases, projects stall after a good start, partners change, or a host of other things happen that one didn't expect. In situations in which the student-evaluator is placed in an agency or group to work as an internal evaluator, the experience could very well turn out to be not as rich as expected.

To address some of these issues, instructors have used case studies in their classes to assist in teaching program evaluation. Although the author is not suggesting that case studies by themselves will rectify the difficulties just noted or serve as a replacement for real-world experiences, they do allow evaluators-in-training to vicariously experience an evaluation project from beginning to end, and case studies place these evaluators in decision-making situations that they otherwise might not be able to experience. Case studies also provide opportunities for rich discussion and learning, while ensuring that certain learning objectives desired by the instructor are achieved.

Until now, the effort to use case studies in teaching program evaluation has been mainly a grass-roots initiative, with instructors bringing into class examples of evaluation projects that they themselves have worked on and putting them into a context for their students. Although the use of case studies and case study books is evident in certain disciplines (such as child and adolescent development), "the absence of readily available teaching cases has been a significant gap in the field of evaluation" (Patton & Patrizi, 2005, p. 1).

The purpose of this book is to provide a variety of evaluation projects to be discussed, analyzed, and reflected on. The case studies are intended to foster rich discussions about evaluation practices, and the book's comprehensive scope means the user can also include discussions of practices touching on real issues that arise when conducting an evaluation project.

For the instructor, this book is not meant to be a stand-alone text for teaching and learning about program evaluation. Its main purpose is to be used as an educational supplement to any course—introductory or advanced—in program evaluation. In addition, these cases should not be viewed as examples of exemplary program evaluations. Although the methods and tools provided with the cases closely reflect those used in the actual evaluations, classroom discussions and activities could certainly focus on expanding and improving those tools and overall methodologies.

Lastly, the case studies presented in this book are a composite of my work in program evaluation over the last decade. When I started to flesh out the dozen or so case studies that eventually came to make up this book, I was challenged by the issue of participant privacy—maintaining the confidentiality that I had promised program participants when I originally conducted the evaluation projects. Would the real people recognize themselves? *Would people remember? Would people even care?* These questions would plague me as I started to construct each case study. These were very serious questions, similar to the serious kinds of questions that professional evaluators have to answer for themselves on a day-to-day basis when working in the field. (They are similar, in fact, to the confidentiality issues faced by the evaluator in Case Study Six.) But from the very beginning it became quite clear to me that to do this I would not be able take a single evaluation project that I had conducted and assemble it into a quick and easy case study. To address this issue, I ended up reflecting on several different projects (sometimes across similar programming, other times not) and dissecting them into dilemmas or scenarios. These dilemmas became the seeds around which I built the case studies. The evaluators and characters in each case study are fictional, though I did base a few characters on composites of fellow evaluators whom I have worked with and admired over the past ten years. And although the programs that are being evaluated are all real programs, the activities and events that unfold around them are fictitious as well.

I hope you enjoy reading these cases and discussing them as much as I have enjoyed revisiting these wonderful experiences myself.

ACKNOWLEDGMENTS

In writing this book I reviewed and reflected on over one hundred program evaluations that I have conducted in the last ten years. This exercise was wonderful in that it brought back many faces of people I have worked with in the past, reminding me of the incredible opportunity I have had to work with some talented evaluators and project managers in the field. I would like to thank all of them for their dedication and hard work in delivering quality programming. I would like specifically to thank Anthony Cardamone, for his technical assistance and feedback concerning school-related issues and school law, and Patricia Ranney, whose enthusiasm for each case got me to write the next one. In addition, I would like to express my thanks to my colleagues in the Educational Psychology Department at the College of Saint Rose, who once again had to endure another book being written, and to Dr. Dianna L. Newman, University of New York at Albany/SUNY, who ten years ago took a chance on a master's student and introduced me to the wonderful field of program evaluation.

For Mr. Mugs,
my laptop-lapdog

THE AUTHOR

Dr. Dean T. Spaulding is an associate professor at the College of Saint Rose in the Department of Educational Psychology. He is the former chair for Teaching Program Evaluation for the American Evaluation Association. He is also one of the authors of *Methods in Educational Research: From Theory to Practice* (Jossey-Bass, 2006). Dr. Spaulding has served as a professional evaluator for more than a decade and has worked extensively in K–12 and higher education settings. Although his work has primarily focused on after-school, enrichment, and mentoring programs, he has also worked to evaluate programs in public health, mental health, and special education at both the state and federal level.

PROGRAM EVALUATION IN PRACTICE

PART

1

INTRODUCTION

CHAPTER

1

FOUNDATIONS OF PROGRAM EVALUATION

After reading the introduction you should be able to

1. Provide a basic definition of program evaluation
2. Understand the different activities conducted by a program evaluator
3. Understanding the difference between formative and summative evaluation
4. Understand the difference between internal and external evaluation

PROGRAM EVALUATION VIGNETTE

An urban school district receives a three-year grant to implement an after-school program to improve student academic achievement. As staff start to implement the program, the district administrator realizes that an evaluation of their program is required. The district administrator also realizes that such work requires expertise of someone from outside the district, and the superintendent, with permission from the school board, hires an external evaluator from a local college. After reviewing the grant, the evaluator conducts an initial review of the program's curriculum and activities. Next the evaluator develops an evaluation plan and presents it at the next school board meeting. The evaluation plan overviews the objectives that the evaluator has developed and the tools that he will use to collect the data. As part of the data collection process the evaluator discusses how the plan will provide two different types of feedback. Formative evaluation will be used to address issues as the program is happening. For example, one question might be: *Are all the stakeholders aware of the program and its offerings?* Summative evaluation will be used to answer the overall evaluation question: *Did students in the after-school program have a significant increase in their academic achievement over those students who did not participate?*

The board approves the plan and the evaluator spends the following month collecting data for the formative and summative portions of the project.

At the next board meeting the evaluator presents some of the formative evaluation and reports that there is a need to increase communication with parents. He suggests that the program increase the number of fliers that are sent home, update the school website, and work more collaboratively with the parent council. In addition, he notes that there is a wide variation in parent education levels within the district and that a large number of parents speak Spanish as their native language. The evaluator recommends that phone calls be made to parents and that all materials be translated into Spanish.

At the end of project year one, summative findings are presented in a final report. The report shows that lack of parent communication is still a problem, and there is little difference in the scores on the standardized measures used to gauge academic achievement of those students who participated in the program and those comparable students who did not participate.

Based on the evaluation report, district officials decide to make modifications to the program for the upcoming year. A parent center, which was not part of the original plan, is added, in the belief this will help increase parent involvement. In addition, the administration decides to cut back on the number of extracurricular activities the after-school program is offering and to focus more on tutoring and academic interventions, hoping that this will increase academic achievement in year two.

WHAT IS PROGRAM EVALUATION?

A common definition used to separate program evaluation from research is that program evaluation is conducted for decision-making purposes, whereas research is intended to build our general understanding and knowledge of a particular topic and to inform practice. In general, program evaluation examines programs to determine their worth and to make recommendations for programmatic refinement and success. Although such a broad definition makes it difficult for those who have not been involved in program evaluation to get a better understanding, it is hoped that the above vignette highlighted some of the activities unique to program evaluation. Let's look a little more closely at some of those activities as we continue this comparison between program evaluation and research.

What Is a Program?

One distinguishing characteristic of program evaluation is that it examines *programs*. A program is a set of specific activities designed for an intended purpose, with quantifiable goals and objectives. Although a research study could certainly examine a particular program, most research tends to be interested in either generalizing findings back to a wider audience (that is, quantitative research) or discussing how the study's findings relate back to the literature (that is, qualitative research). Most research studies, especially those that are quantitative, are not interested in knowing how just one after-school program functioned in one school building or district. However, for those conducting program evaluations this is seen as precisely the purpose.

Programs come in many different shapes and sizes, and therefore so do the evaluations that are conducted. Educational programs can take place anytime during the school day or after. For example, programs can include a morning breakfast/nutrition program, a high-school science program, an after-school program, or even a weekend program. Educational programs do not necessarily have to occur on school grounds. An evaluator may conduct an evaluation of a community group's educational program or a program at the local YMCA or Boys and Girls Club.

Accessing the Setting and Participants

Another characteristic that sets program evaluation apart from research is the difference in how the program evaluator and the researcher gain access to the project and program site. As described in the vignette, the program evaluator was hired by the school district to conduct the evaluation of their after-school program. In general, a program evaluator enters into a contractual agreement either directly or indirectly with the group whose program is being evaluated. This individual or group is often referred to as the *client*.

Because of this relationship between the program evaluator and the client, the scope of what the evaluator wishes to look at could also be restricted by the client. To have the client dictate what one will investigate for a research study would be very unusual. For example, because of the nature of qualitative research, a qualitative researcher who enters a school system to do a study on school safety may find a gang present in the school and choose to follow the experience of students as they try to leave the gang. If a program evaluation was conducted in the same school, the evaluator might be aware of the gang and students trying to get out of the gang, and this might strike the evaluator as an interesting phenomenon, but the evaluator would not pursue it unless the client perceived it as an important aspect of school safety or unless gang control fit into the original objectives of the program.

Collecting and Using Data

As demonstrated in the vignette, program evaluation often collects two different forms of evaluation data: *formative* and *summative*. A further discussion about formative and summative evaluation is presented later in this chapter; essentially, the purpose of formative data is to change or make better the very thing that is being studied (at the very moment in which it is being studied). This is typically not found in most applied research approaches. Rarely would the researcher have this reporting relationship, whereby formative findings are reported back to stakeholders or participants for the purposes of immediately changing the program.

Changing Practice

Although program evaluation uses the same methods as research to collect data, program evaluation is different from research in its overall purpose or intent, as well as the speed at which it changes practice. The overall purpose of applied research (for example, correlational, case study, experimental) is to expand our general understanding or knowledge about the topic and ultimately to inform practice. Although gathering empirical evidence that supports a new method or approach is certainly a main purpose of applied research, this doesn't necessarily mean that people will suddenly abandon what they have been doing for years and switch to the research-supported approach.

In the vignette, we can see that change occurred much more rapidly through the use of program evaluation. Based on the evaluation report, administrators, school board members, and project staff decided to reconfigure the structure of the after-school program and to provide parents with a center in the hope of increasing parent involvement. In addition, it was also decided that many of the extracurricular activities would be eliminated and that the new focus would be on the tutorial component of the program—hoping to see even more improvement in students' academic scores in the coming year.

For another example, consider applied research in the area of instructional methods in literacy. In the 1980s, the favored instructional approach was whole language; however, a decade of research began to support another approach: phonics. Despite the mounting evidence in favor of phonics, it took approximately a decade for practitioners to change their instruction. In the early 1990s, however, researchers began to examine the benefits of using both whole language and phonics in what is referred to as a *blended approach*. Again, despite substantial empirical evidence, it took another ten years for many practitioners to use both approaches in their classrooms. This is admittedly a simplified version of what occurred; the purpose here is to show the relationship between applied research and practice in the speed (or lack of speed) with which systems or settings that they evaluate implement changes, based on applied research.

Although there are certainly many program evaluations after which resulting changes do not occur swiftly (or at all), one difference between program evaluation and research is the increased emphasis that program evaluation places on the occurrence of such change. In fact, there are philosophies and approaches in program evaluation that so emphasize the use of evaluation findings that they believe if the evaluation report and recommendations are not used by program staff to make decisions and changes to the program, the entire evaluation was a complete waste of time, energy, and resources (Patton, 1997).

Reporting Findings and Recommendations

Another feature of program evaluation that separates it from research is the way in which program evaluation findings are presented. In conducting empirical research it is common practice for the researcher to write a study for publication—preferably in a high-level refereed journal. In program evaluation, as shown in the vignette, the findings are presented in what is commonly referred to as the evaluation report, not through publishing in a journal. In addition, the majority of evaluation reports are given directly to the group or client that has hired the evaluator to perform the work and are not made available to others.

Formative and Summative Evaluation

Both quantitative and qualitative data can be collected in program evaluation. Depending on the purpose of and the audience for the evaluation, an evaluator may choose to conduct an evaluation that is solely quantitative or solely qualitative or a mixed-methods approach. In addition to using quantitative and qualitative data, a program evaluator also has the option of providing summative and formative evaluation within a project (see Figure 1.1).

The choice of whether to conduct a summative or a formative evaluation is not exclusively dictated by whether the evaluator collects quantitative or qualitative data. Many people have the misperception that summative evaluation uses exclusively quantitative data and qualitative data is used for formative evaluation. This is not always the case. Whether evaluation feedback is formative or summative depends on what type of information it is and when it is provided to the client (see Figure 1.1).

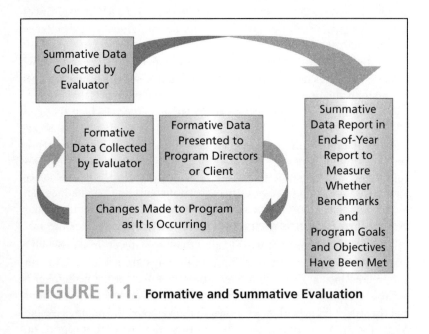

FIGURE 1.1. Formative and Summative Evaluation

Data for summative evaluation is collected for the purpose of measuring outcomes and how those outcomes relate to the overall judgment of the program and its success. As demonstrated in the vignette, summative findings are provided to the client at the end of the project or at the end of the project year or cycle. Typically, summative data includes student scores on standardized measures such as state assessments, intelligence tests, and content-area tests. Surveys and qualitative data gathered through interviews with stakeholders may also serve as summative data if the questions or items are designed to elicit participant responses that summarize their perceptions of outcomes or experiences.

For example, an interview question that asks participants to discuss any academic or behavioral changes that they have seen in students as a result of participating in the after-school program will gather summative information. This information would be reported in an end-of-project-year report. However, an interview question that asks stakeholders to discuss any improvements *that could be made* to the program to better assist students in reaching those intended outcomes will gather formative information.

Formative data is different from summative in that rather than being collected from participants at the end of the project to measure outcomes, formative data is collected and reported back to project staff as the program is taking place. Data gathered for formative evaluation must be reported back to the client in a timely manner. There is little value in formative evaluation when the evaluator does not report such findings to the client until the project is over. Formative evaluation feedback can be reported through the use of memos, presentations, or even phone calls. The important role of formative feedback is to identify and address the issues or serious problems in the project. Imagine if the evaluator in our vignette did not report back formative findings regarding parent communication. How many students might not have been able to participate in the after-school activities? One of the evaluator's tasks is to identify these program barriers, then inform program staff so that changes can occur. When programs are being implemented for the first time, formative feedback is especially important to developers and staff. Some programs require several years of intense formative feedback to get the kinks out before the program can become highly successful.

Formative feedback and the use of that information to change or improve the program is one factor that separates program evaluation from most types of applied research approaches. Classical experimental or quasi-experimental research approaches attempt to control for extraneous variables so that only the independent variable can affect the dependant variable. An important aspect of experimental research is a clear definition of the different treatments or level of independent variable. If the program itself is the treatment variable, then it must be designed before the study begins. An experimental researcher would consider it disastrous if formative feedback were given because the treatment was changed in the middle of the study. In contrast, program evaluators, while trying to keep the independent variables or treatment constant, realize that it is better to make modifications to the program—even if it "distorts" the lines of causality—than to deliver a substandard program consistently for the entire school year.

Training in Program Evaluation

Many students wonder *How do evaluators get involved in program evaluation?* and *Where do they receive their training?* These are both good questions. Although program evaluation today is certainly a much more recognized field, it is made up of both those who have formal training in program evaluation theory and practices as well as those who have been less formally trained. There is no specialized degree or certification required for people to call themselves evaluators. Today a number of colleges and universities offer course work in program evaluation as well as advanced degrees in this area. Although course work will vary by institution, most focuses on quantitative and qualitative methods, program evaluation theory, and ethics, as well as a practicum experience.

As in any field, program evaluators come from a wide range of backgrounds and experiences as well as different philosophical and methodological perspectives. Often faculty at colleges and universities serve as program evaluation consultants working with area school districts, agencies, non-profit and not-for-profit programs, and other institutions of higher education. There are also private evaluation consulting companies that hire program evaluators. Furthermore, public agencies at both the state and federal level also hire program evaluators for full-time positions to conduct internal evaluations in that setting, as well as to conduct single- and multisite evaluations.

The American Evaluation Association is an international organization devoted to improving evaluation practices and methods, increasing its use, promoting evaluation as a profession, and supporting evaluation to generate theory and knowledge. This organization has approximately four thousand members and representatives from fifty states and sixty countries. Each year the association hosts an annual conference in the United States that focuses on a theme, such as collaboration, methodology, or utilization (see http://www.eval.org/News/news.htm).The association also comprises special interest groups (SIGs) that specialize in certain areas or topics, such as teaching program evaluation or environmental evaluation.

INTERNAL AND EXTERNAL EVALUATORS

The proximity of an evaluator to what is being evaluated certainly plays a critical role in both the access to information, the collection of that information, and the reporting and use of that information to promote change. Just as the waiter at a restaurant has a very different perspective on the food and the management from that of the food critic who comes to dine and to write up a review for the local paper, an evaluator's perspective on and relationship to the setting or program must be considered. In the field of program evaluation, this perspective is often addressed by what are referred to as *internal* and *external evaluators*. An external evaluator is someone from outside the immediate setting who is hired to come in and evaluate the program. Since this person has no obligations, in theory he or she has no immediate biases for or against the program or any one of the stakeholder groups involved in the project. Most programs that receive federal, state, or foundation funding require an external evaluator to be present.

On the other hand, many companies, agencies, institutes of higher education, school districts, and other groups also employ internal evaluators. An internal evaluator is typically an employee of the company, agency, or group who is responsible for carrying out duties that pertain to evaluation. For example, many school districts now have a program evaluator on staff. This person is responsible for establishing and working with databases to maintain student academic and behavioral data and using data to assist staff and administration in improving practice. Internal evaluators at districts provide expertise in working with the state testing and accountability data, as well as monitoring programs that the school is currently implementing.

There are many strengths—and many barriers—to the use of both internal and external evaluators. As mentioned earlier, the main reason that many funding agencies require an external evaluator to be present is to increase the objectivity of the data collection. This may or may not be achieved; however, the external evaluator also inevitably encounters some barriers. External evaluators are often faced with the difficulty of establishing trust with the stakeholders involved in the program that they are evaluating. Even though the external evaluator is collecting data on the program and not specifically on the performance of program staff, this stakeholder group may not welcome the evaluator with open arms. Stakeholders may, and often do, see the evaluator as a threat—someone whose job it is to find "holes" in the program. They may see the evaluator's work as a direct threat to their livelihood. In some cases the stakeholders may feel that the external evaluator "really doesn't know us" or "doesn't know what we are all about." In some cases, they may feel that the evaluator doesn't know enough about the setting or the context of how things work in that setting to be able to gather in-depth data that would pertain to them and be meaningful for evaluation purposes. In many cases, stakeholders who are uncertain about this evaluator are likely to avoid the evaluator altogether, not returning phone calls to set up interviews or not returning surveys. It is a daunting and often difficult challenge for even the most seasoned of program evaluators to enter a foreign setting, establish trust with the various groups involved in the program, and provide meaningful data back to participants for programmatic improvements.

Internal evaluators typically do not have to deal with gaining the trust of stakeholders as external evaluators do. In addition, internal evaluators know the setting, how to access needed data, and the "language" that each group uses. In some cases both an internal and an external evaluator are retained. If an internal evaluator is already present in a school system or program, then an evaluation plan should encompass the work of both evaluators to optimize the breadth and depth of data collected and, ideally, to ensure the overall success of the program. In such situations, the internal evaluator would be responsible for collecting certain types of data to which the external evaluator would not have access. In turn, the external evaluator would collect additional data to ensure the authenticity and objectivity of the evaluation effort and its findings.

TYPES OR MODELS OF PROGRAM EVALUATION

Just as there are many types of applied research approaches, there are several different approaches that program evaluators can use. The most common approach to program evaluation is the *objective-based approach,* which uses objectives written by both the creators of the program and the evaluator. An evaluation objective is a written statement that depicts the overarching purpose of the evaluation and clearly states the type of information that will be collected. Often these objectives are further supported through the use of *benchmarks*. A benchmark is more detailed than an objective in that it specifically states what quantitative goals the participants in the program need to reach for the program to be successful. Box 1.1 presents an evaluation objective followed by a program benchmark.

BOX 1.1. **Example of an Evaluation Objective and Benchmark**

Evaluation Objective: To document middle school student changes in academic achievement, particularly in the area of reading and literacy skills.

Benchmark: Students in grades fifth through eighth will show a 10 percent gain on the ELA state assessment in year one and a 20 percent increase in students passing the ELA in program years two and three.

Evaluators will often start with the objectives for the evaluation and build evaluation data collection activities from those objectives. Evaluation objectives may guide either formative or summative data collection. Either way, quantitative or qualitative data, or both, are collected and findings are compared to the project's objectives. Objectives are certainly helpful in shaping the evaluation, but there is a risk that evaluators may become so focused on the objectives that they lose sight of other unanticipated outcomes or benefits to participants as a result of the program.

Although objectives assist in guiding an evaluation, there is another method—the *goal-free evaluation* approach—that doesn't prescribe using evaluation objectives. This approach is guided by the perspective that there are many findings and outcomes that do not fall within the strict confines of the goals and objectives established by both the project directors and the evaluator. Those who practice goal-free evaluation believe that the unforeseen outcomes may be more important than outcomes that the program developers employ. One difficulty in conducting a goal-free evaluation is that projects that receive funding are required to show specific outcomes based on objectives. If the outcomes are not included in the evaluation, the appropriate data may not be collected.

The *expertise-oriented evaluation* approach—one of the oldest and most frequently used methods of program evaluation—employs the evaluator to be a content expert and to serve more as judge than as evaluator

(Fitzpatrick, Sanders, & Worthen, 2004). Agencies granting accreditation to institutions, program, or services send program evaluators to these sites to conduct an expertise-oriented evaluation. In these situations, typically data are not collected by the evaluators but are presented to them by those participants being judged or seeking accreditation. With this approach, the evaluators judge the program or service based on an established set of criteria as well as their own expertise in the area. An example of this type of evaluation is the National Council for Accreditation of Teacher Education (NCATE). Colleges and universities who train teachers often seek national accreditation to demonstrate the quality of their programs.

The *participatory-oriented evaluation* approach uses a very different perspective on program evaluation than the other approaches described so far. Whereas those approaches focus on the program and examining different aspects of the program, the participatory-oriented evaluation approach is ultimately interested in those whom the program serves. Using this model, the evaluator will seek to involve program participants in the evaluation of the program. In some cases the participants will develop instruments, collect data, analyze data, and report findings.

HOW TO USE THIS BOOK

To provide some standardization, a framework was developed and applied to each case study in this book. Box 1.2 presents an overview of the framework sections and a brief explanation of each.

ADDITIONAL RESOURCES

As we can see, there are many different approaches to conducting an evaluation of a program. It should be noted that although the objective-based approach is not the sole approach for conducting an evaluation, because of federal and state funding and the focus on meeting goals and benchmarks in today's climate of accountability, it is, generally speaking, the most widely used approach. In addition, an objective-based evaluation will most likely be the first type of evaluation that a new evaluator just entering the trade will be exposed to and have to conduct. Therefore, most of the case studies presented in this book follow a more objective-based approach.

This section presents some additional resources and readings to assist those who are relatively new to program evaluation and to more

BOX 1.2 Overview of Framework to Guide Each Case Study

The Evaluator
In this section the evaluator or evaluators are introduced. The role of the evaluator is also discussed here, as well as the evaluator's background, education, and connection to the evaluation project as a whole.

The Program
Here the program that is being evaluated is described: its purpose, its implementation, and relevant stakeholders and participants. In addition, where possible, the goals and objectives of the program as well as the program's structure and design are overviewed.

The Evaluation Plan
Here the evaluator's evaluation plan is discussed in as much detail as possible. This includes but is not limited to the objectives that are driving the evaluation and the methods and tools that the evaluator is using or plans to use to conduct the evaluation.

Summary of Evaluation Activities and Findings
This section describes the data collection process of the evaluation and a summary or overview of any evaluation findings from the evaluation. In each of the cases, the evaluator(s) are usually presented with a dilemma or situation at the end of this section.

Final Thoughts
This section provides the reader with a conclusion: what really happened at the end of the evaluation, how the evaluator handled the dilemma, and the results of those actions for the evaluator and the project as a whole.

clearly delineate some of the activities overviewed and described in each case study.

The Evaluation Objective

In an objective-based evaluation approach, the evaluation objective is the cornerstone of conducting a rigorous and successful evaluation project. Evaluation objectives are written goals under which the evaluation data will be collected and reported. Box 1.3 presents a list of evaluation objectives used in evaluating the summer camp project.

BOX 1.3 **Evaluation Objectives for a Summer Camp Project**

Objective 1: To document stakeholder perceptions as to the purpose of the camp.

Objective 2: To document activities conducted during camp.

Objective 3: To document stakeholder perceptions of the lessons learned and the strengths and barriers of the camp.

Objective 4: To document student outcomes as a result of participating in the camp.

Objective 5: To document modifications made to programming based on the previous year's evaluation recommendations.

The typical evaluation has four or five main evaluation objectives. Specific data are collected to answer or address each evaluation objective. For many grant-funded projects evaluation objectives are already established and clearly defined in the grant. In such cases, an evaluator must work with the established objectives and begin to develop an evaluation matrix (see the following section). However, for projects with no pre-established evaluation objectives, the evaluator must play a significant role in their development.

Developing evaluation objectives in a collaborative setting can be a useful tool for an evaluator to use. To both build trust and gain buy-in from the different stakeholder groups (such as teachers, staff, administrators, parents), it is helpful to gather representatives from all parties for a discussion about the goals of the project and what outcomes or results they believe a program such as this would produce.

It should also be noted that evaluation objectives are not static; they can change over time. There may be objectives deemed important in the very beginning of a multiyear evaluation that are not emphasized at the end of the project. Typically, formative evaluation objectives (discussed shortly) are emphasized in the early stages of the evaluation timeline, and summative evaluation objectives (also discussed shortly) take on a more realistic and important role toward the end of the project.

No matter what objectives and timelines are being used, it is imperative that evaluation objectives are aligned to the project goals and activities. For example, let's say that the main focus of a summer enrichment program is literacy. As part of the program's activities, students or campers keep journals, work with local storytellers to author their own stories, and receive tutoring or interventions in literacy. From this experience project developers and staff hope that students will become more interested in reading and literacy as a whole and that this enthusiasm will eventually flow over to students' increasing their performance on some standardized reading measure they take at a later point. From this single program component, two evaluation objectives could potentially be developed, such as these two possibilities:

■ *To document an increase in students' interest in and frequency of engaging in reading and other literacy-based activities.* Data for this evaluation objective could be collected through pre-post interviews with students documenting whether they believe their interest in and frequency of such practices has increased over time as a result of participating in the project. Supporting evidence could also be collected from parents, who may be observing their child reading more books at night, taking more books out of the library, talking about the book they are reading at dinner, and so on. An analysis of student campers' journals, the list of books they have completed, book reports, and so on could serve as additional evidence to support these claims.

The second objective could focus on more "hard" or end outcomes (such as test scores). A discussion of end outcomes is presented later in this section.

■ *To document increases in student performance on a standardized literacy measure administered annually.* This objective would require the evaluator to obtain students' scores on the annual measure to determine whether there appears to be any relationship between students participating in the program and scores increasing on the assessment.

Evaluation objectives will vary somewhat depending on the program. However, there are some general categories that all objectives can fall under. Box 1.4 presents a description of those categories.

BOX 1.4. General Categories of Evaluation Objectives

Documenting Activities. Objectives such as these work toward documenting what the program "looks like" by describing what activities took place. Data for these types of objectives can be gathered through interviews, focus groups, or surveys (see "Tools for Collecting Data" later in this introduction), and through direct observations of program activities.

Documenting Program Implementation. These objectives focus on documenting processes associated with program start-up and basic program implementation. As part of this effort the evaluator would be interested in documenting strengths as well as barriers to program implementation. For example, one barrier might be that the evaluator discovers there isn't enough busing available for everyone who wants to attend field trips. Barriers that severely impact the quality of the programming (such as an instructor not using the correct curriculum) should be documented and fed back immediately to the project director so this problem can be corrected in a timely manner. Safety concerns are another barrier that requires immediate feedback. Again, evaluation in which information is presented to staff in a timely fashion is *formative*. Because of its timely nature, formative evaluation findings are often reported to program staff through the use of memorandum reports and presentations. These presentations can be done at the project's weekly or monthly meetings.

Documenting Outputs of Activities. These objectives focus on outputs or changes that occur as a result of some activity. These changes tend to be associated with what people *believe* or how they *perform* or *act*. For example, if program staff attended a seminar on working with at-risk students and as a result of engaging in this activity their beliefs about poverty changed or they changed some aspect of their instruction, this would qualify as a finding that would meet this objective. Data for these types of objectives can be gathered through interviews and surveys. Before using a survey to document these outputs, the evaluator should allow some time to pass between participating in the seminar and returning to the classroom. For an example of an output of activity objective, see the first of the previous set of two example objectives, *"To document an increase in students' interest in and frequency of engaging in reading and other literacy-based activities."*

Documenting End Outcomes. These objectives focus on documenting changes in the participants themselves. In after-school and enrichment programs these end outcomes are often referred to as *hard outcomes*—that is, outcomes that are measured with a standardized measure or assessment; for example, changes in students' reading, math, or science scores on a standardized measure are considered to be end outcomes. A decrease in the number of violent incidences, increase in student attendance, and increase in student coursework grades could also be used to satisfy end outcome evaluation objectives.

Designing and Developing an Evaluation Matrix

One of the first activities to be conducted during the planning of the evaluation is the development of an evaluation matrix. The matrix serves as a blueprint to guide the evaluator and to ensure that all necessary data are collected. Table 1.1 presents an example of a matrix used to evaluate the summer camp project. Although each project will have its own unique evaluation objectives, the basic components essential to all evaluations are the same. Notice in the example matrix shown that the evaluation is being guided by five individual objectives. Notice also that the matrix contains the timeline for when the data will be collected and the methods and measurement tools the evaluator intends to use for data collection, and it specifies whether the data are summative (findings presented at the end of the project) or formative (findings presented as the project is occurring). The more detail the evaluator can present in the matrix, the easier it will be to conduct and carry out the overall evaluation. Most evaluators use some sort of matrix, even though it may not be spelled out as formally as the one in the table.

In addition to helping organize the evaluation, the evaluation matrix is also a wonderful tool in helping the evaluator build trust with the various stakeholder groups involved in the project. In doing so, evaluators may have early discussions with representatives from individual stakeholder groups (such as teachers, parents, staff) about the data collection process and the kinds of information that stakeholders perceive as important and useful. It is recommended that the evaluator incorporate the assistance and feedback from all stakeholders into the building of the evaluation matrix before data are collected. Keep in mind that on a multiyear project, the matrix and data collection activities are likely to change slightly as new objectives are added to the evaluation plan and old objectives that have been met and no longer need to be monitored are done away with.

Tools for Collecting Data

As specified in the evaluation matrix, the tools that the evaluator uses to collect data will vary depending on several factors, including the size of the stakeholder group, the educational or developmental level of the stakeholder group, and the evaluator's access to the stakeholder group. This section presents a few of the basic tools commonly used by evaluators and typical methodologies used for evaluations of after-school, summer, and enrichment-oriented programs.

TABLE 1.1. Evaluation Matrix for Summer Camp

Evaluation Objective	Stakeholder Group	Tools Used to Collect Data	When	Purpose
Evaluation Objective One: To document the depth and breadth of activities provided during follow-up session (2004–2005)	Faculty and project directors and campers	Interview	July	Summative
Evaluation Objective Two: To document student satisfaction with the follow-up activities	Students	Interview and observations	Now	Summative
	Parents	Post-survey	March–April	Summative
Evaluation Objective Three: To document faculty perceptions of the follow-up activities	Faculty and project director	Interviews	March–April	Summative
Evaluation Objective Four: To document parent perceptions of student outcomes from participating in camp and follow-up activities	Parents	Survey	March–April	Summative
Evaluation Objective Five: To document changes in student learning and abilities	Students	Word knowledge assessment	March 5 (post)	Summative

Data Sources

Surveys or self-report measures. The survey or self-report measure is perhaps the most common data collection tool used by program evaluators. One reason this tool is so popular is the overall ease with which surveys can be administered. Surveys are usually administered through a mail-out, mail-back procedure; however, in some cases they may be collected on-site, typically following an activity such as a workshop or an information session.

Surveys can be administered across multiple groups involved in a program. Keep in mind that in doing so, wording of items may need to be modified slightly for the different groups. The following is a list of stakeholders that the evaluator may want to consider surveying when conducting an evaluation of an after-school, enrichment-oriented, or summer program.

- Parents and guardians

- Project administrators

- Project staff

- Parents

- Community members, volunteers, senior citizens

- Students

- Presenters and service providers

Designing a Survey

When designing the survey it is important that the final form of the survey be piloted or field tested prior to being sent out, to ensure that there are no errors in the survey that would keep participants from being able to properly fill it out. In addition, it is important to be aware of possible language or reading ability barriers for those being surveyed. Pretesting the survey with a handful of those participants should give the evaluator an accurate idea of how the survey will perform when administered to the entire stakeholder group.

Exhibit 1.1 presents a survey designed to gather information from parents and guardians of the students participating in the project. The survey was specifically developed to address multiple evaluation objectives.

EXHIBIT 1.1. Parent or Guardian Perception Survey—Summer Camp

PLEASE RETURN by July 30

As part of the effort to evaluate the summer camp, the following survey has been designed to gather your perceptions regarding the activities associated with the camp. The information that you provide will assist in delivering important formative feedback to program coordinators and to the granting agency, as well as help in meeting the intended objectives and outcomes of the overall project. Your responses are confidential and will not be shared with anyone in any way that identifies you as an individual. Only aggregated data will be presented in the final evaluation report. Your participation in this survey process is completely voluntary and will not impact your child's future attendance in the program. Your time and cooperation are greatly appreciated. If you have any questions regarding this survey or the overall process please contact Dr. Dean T. Spaulding, Assistant Professor, Department of Educational Psychology, College of Saint Rose, Albany, NY 12203, (518) 454-2865 or e-mail at Spauldid@strose.edu

Please have the parent or guardian who had the most involvement with camp complete this survey.

Perceptions of Recruitment

The following items seek to gather your perceptions regarding your overall beliefs about the recruitment process for summer camp. Please read each item carefully and use the scale below to show your level of agreement with each item.

1=Strongly Disagree 2=Disagree 3=Slightly Disagree 4=Slightly Agree 5=Agree 6=Strongly Agree

I was provided with camp information in a timely fashion. 1 2 3 4 5 6

The program brochure provided me with a way to get
additional information prior to enrollment. 1 2 3 4 5 6

I found the enrollment process to be easy. 1 2 3 4 5 6

How did you hear about camp? _____

Perceptions of Orientation

The following items are designed to gather your perceptions about the orientation process for summer camp. Please read each item carefully and use the scale below to show your level of agreement with each item.

1=Strongly Disagree 2=Disagree 3=Slightly Disagree 4=Slightly Agree 5=Agree 6=Strongly Agree

I believe the check-in process at orientation was
well organized. 1 2 3 4 5 6

| I left orientation feeling confident that my child was in good hands. | 1 2 3 4 5 6 |

I left orientation feeling confident that my child was in good hands.　1 2 3 4 5 6

I believe dinner at orientation allowed me to meet the counselors/teachers my child would be working with.　1 2 3 4 5 6

I think having dinner with my child at orientation allowed me to be included in the camp experience.　1 2 3 4 5 6

The information session at orientation provided me with a clear understanding of what my child would be doing at summer camp.　1 2 3 4 5 6

I was encouraged to participate in camp activities throughout the ten-day program.　1 2 3 4 5 6

I was provided contact numbers and information.　1 2 3 4 5 6

I was provided enough information so I could attend camp activities and field trips.　1 2 3 4 5 6

Food was appropriate for children.　1 2 3 4 5 6

I enjoyed the Hudson River Rambler performance.　1 2 3 4 5 6

If you went to the dorms with your child either on orientation night or visited at a later date, please answer the next three questions:

I left the dorms feeling my child was in a safe place.　1 2 3 4 5 6

I felt the house was clean.　1 2 3 4 5 6

I felt the room would be a comfortable place for my child.　1 2 3 4 5 6

Perceptions of Parent Involvement During Camp

If you participated in the following activities, indicate your participation with a ✓:

Date	Breakfast	AM Session	Lunch	PM Session	Dinner	Field Trip
Monday 7/5						
Tuesday 7/6						
Wednesday 7/7						
Thursday 7/8						
Friday 7/9						
Saturday 7/10						
Sunday 7/11						
Monday 7/12						
Tuesday 7/13						
Wednesday 7/14						
Thursday 7/15						

(Exhibit 1.1 continued)

If you did not participate in any or all of the activities on the front page, please circle your reason (circle all that apply):

A. I did not have transportation.

B. I had other child care needs.

C. I had work conflicts.

D. I thought I would have to pay to participate.

E. I was not interested.

F. I did not know I could participate.

G. Other _____

_____

Reflections of Camp

From what you have heard or observed from your child, what did your child like about summer camp? (check all that apply)

___Food   ___Dorm room   ___Class time

___Field trips   ___Counselors   ___Teachers/Professors

___Night activities ___Speakers/Guest lecturer ___Other campers

___Campers' cameras ___Final presentations   ___Working on the computers

Other (please explain): _____

From what you have heard or observed from your child, what didn't your child like about Summer Camp? (check all that apply)

___Food   ___Dorm room   ___Class time

___Field trips   ___Counselors   ___Teachers/Professors

___Night activities ___Speakers/Guest lecturer ___Other campers

___Campers' cameras ___Final presentations   ___Working on the computers

Other (please explain): _____

1=Strongly Disagree 2=Disagree 3=Slightly Disagree 4=Slightly Agree 5=Agree 6=Strongly Agree

I believe my child wants to come back to camp.	1 2 3 4 5 6
My expectations of camp were met.	1 2 3 4 5 6
I believe my child's expectations of camp were met.	1 2 3 4 5 6

Perceptions of Impact on Academics/School

The following items are designed to gather your perceptions about the possible impact attending camp may make on your child's academics and school-related work in the upcoming school year. Please read each item carefully and use the scale below to indicate your level of agreement with each item.

1=Strongly Disagree 2=Disagree 3=Slightly Disagree 4=Slightly Agree 5=Agree 6=Strongly Agree

I believe that this camp experience will help my child in school.	1	2	3	4	5	6
My child has been continuing activities experienced at camp.	1	2	3	4	5	6
I have noticed improvement in the way my child interacts with other children.	1	2	3	4	5	6
I plan to attend the follow-up sessions with my child.	1	2	3	4	5	6
I would be willing to send my child to summer camp next year.	1	2	3	4	5	6
I would recommend summer camp to other parents.	1	2	3	4	5	6

Demographic Items (Optional)

About you (Please check all appropriate items):

School district _____

Grade level (Fall 2003) _____ Child's age _____

Child's gender ____ male ____ female

Did your child attend camp last year? ____ yes ____no

Total number of members within the household? ____
Number of children ____   Number of adults ____

Which camp did your child participate in?
____Storytelling ____American history ____ I don't know

Which residence hall did your child live in?
____Fontebonne____ Charter____McGinn____ I don't know

PLEASE PROVIDE ANY ADDITIONAL COMMENTS:
_____

_____

_____

Other Types of Scales for Collecting Data Through Surveys

A successful survey asks only needed information and is easy and quick to complete. A survey that is too general and appears to be asking questions that have little or nothing to do with the project will quickly be dismissed by those who are expected to fill it out. A survey should collect only data that are essential and needed for the evaluator to complete the evaluation of the project. In addition, the evaluator should know exactly which questions or items on the survey are aligned with which objectives. For example, an evaluator should know that items 4 through 14 will answer evaluation objective one and items 15 through 26 will address objective two, and so on. Planning in such detail will ensure that only essential information is collected. This information can be included in an evaluation matrix.

The following are a few common scales and approaches that can be used to solicit information from participants.

Likert scales. These scales are commonly used in surveys. Respondents are presented with complete statements (for example, "I found the program increased students' interest in reading") and use an agreement scale to indicate their beliefs, selecting the number that best represents how they feel. Here is an example of a Likert scale:

> 1=Strongly Disagree; 2=Disagree; 3=Slightly Disagree;
> 4=Slightly Agree; 5=Agree; 6=Strongly Agree

Checklist. This is an easy way to gather breadth of information from participants. A checklist is essentially a list of possible answers that respondents check off if applicable. Although constructing a checklist is not difficult, generating such breadth of items can sometimes pose difficulties, especially if the evaluator is not fully aware of all the possible answers that would be appropriate. Sometimes conducting a few initial interviews with members from stakeholder groups can help the evaluator expand the checklist to ensure that it gathers valid data. It is also advisable to include an "Other" category at the end of the checklist. This allows respondents to write a response that was not posted on the checklist. (See Exhibit 1.1 for examples of checklists.)

Open-ended or free response. These items ask an open-ended question and expect respondents to give detailed answers. Unlike the other methods just described, open-ended items allow the respondents to describe "how" and "what" in much more depth. However, in constructing a survey it is important not to overuse open-ended questions. Too many open-ended items on a survey can deter participants from filling it out. Open-ended questions should be used appropriately. Data derived from them should be linked directly to answering evaluation objectives, and the evaluator should avoid putting open-ended items at the end of the survey just to fill in any extra blank space.

Demographics. A demographics section can be placed at the beginning or end of a survey to gather personal information about the participants. This information can vary widely depending on the purpose of the project. The survey in Exhibit 1.1 has limited demographics; additional possibilities include gender, age, marital status, years employed in current position, educational level, and annual income.

One-to-One Interviews

Although many of us probably have some idea of how interviews are conducted, we may not realize that they are more than simply asking questions of someone and writing down his or her responses. To have a successful interview requires proper advance planning. The evaluator needs to establish the time and location and develop a protocol or list of questions. These lists are often called *interview protocols*. Typically, an interview protocol contains no more than six to eight open-ended questions. Interviewing with such a list should take about an hour, depending on the project and the level of detail that is needed. As with the other tools, questions from the interview protocol must also be linked to specific evaluation objectives.

Aside from developing six to eight broad questions, the evaluator may also want to develop subquestions or *probes*. Probes help to ensure that specific information within the larger context of the questioning process are being addressed. One of the benefits of using an interview protocol in conducting multiple interviews is that the protocol helps to standardize the process, so everyone is asked the exact same questions, word for word.

Exhibit 1.2 presents an example of an interview protocol that was used for the evaluation of the summer camp. This protocol was used to interview instructors from the summer camp. Questions 3 and 7 provide examples of a subquestion or probe.

Another method of collecting data from stakeholders, the *focus group*, is very similar to one-to-one interviews. To conduct a focus group, the evaluator first develops a protocol—a series of open-ended questions; however, instead of asking them of an individual, the questions are posed to a group of stakeholders for discussion. The advantage of this technique is that often the conversations will get much deeper because of the different perspectives of the assembled individuals.

EXHIBIT 1.2 Interview Protocol

1.   What was the purpose of the follow-up sessions?

2a. What was the overall process for developing the follow-up sessions?

2b. How does that extend and support the curriculum delivered at the summer camp?

3.   Describe the activities used in the follow-up session. Which of these did you find the campers were most and least engaged in?

4.   What do you see as the main learning objectives of the activities?

5.   Overall, have the learning objectives been met? If so, how?

6.   What changes would you make to the curriculum for next year's follow-up?

7a. What changes do you see, if any, in these students in the time you have been working with them?
     • As a group?
     • On an individual student basis?

7b. What other possible changes in students' performance could you expect to see as a result of students participating in this experience?

8.   What do you see as the Saturday follow-up's strengths?

9.   What do you see as barriers?

10a. Has your experience in developing and implementing curriculum for camp and the follow-up sessions changed how you think about or develop curriculum for your college classes?

10b. Has it changed how you instruct others to teach this population?

11. What are some of the lessons you have learned from this experience?

When conducting a focus group, it is important that the evaluator set ground rules beforehand to ensure that all participants respect each other, even if their views on the situation are very different. At least two evaluators should be present when conducting a focus group: one to ask the questions and the other to take notes.

A video or an audio recording device can be used during both interviews and focus groups. This will help to ensure the accuracy of the data being collected by allowing the evaluator to add further detail and quotes that might not otherwise have been recorded. If the evaluator is planning on using such a device, it is important that those being interviewed are informed and agree, both off and on tape.

Alternative Forms of Data

In addition to using surveys and interview protocols, evaluators are always seeking creative ways to collect different kinds of data. Often, when working with school-age children, evaluators will have the students keep journals about their experiences with the project. When considering using journals as a source of data collection, it is important—especially with students in middle school grades—to provide some sort of structure for their journal entries. One way to do this is to provide daily or weekly themes or even questions that students must respond to by writing in their journals. In addition, the evaluator should make it quite clear that the student journals are going to be collected and read as part of the evaluation.

Photography is another excellent method for collecting data. An evaluator who wishes to use photography as an alternative data collection method has several options. First, the evaluator can either choose to be the photographer and photograph students engaging in activities or allow the students to be the photographers. During the summer camp program, campers were each given a disposable camera and asked to photograph things that they liked or didn't like about camp. Over the course of the next ten days campers took lots of pictures during field trips, class time, and free time. Later the photographs were developed and students were interviewed, using their photographs as prompts to further the conversation.

Writing the Evaluation Report

There is no one way to construct an evaluation report, but there are some general guidelines. Typically, summative evaluation reports are written and presented at the end of each project year. In some cases, a midyear project status report is required. As the evaluator you should determine whether such a midyear project is needed and plan accordingly.

The following are the basic sections of an evaluation report:

Cover Page. This should contain the title of the project, the evaluator's name and credentials, the client or name of the organization who commissioned the report, and the date or time of year that the report is being submitted (for example, Summer 2005).

Executive Summary. For short reports, an executive summary is not necessary. Typically, an executive summary runs one or two pages and provides a short purpose and methodology for the report, the essential main findings, a conclusion, and recommendations, if appropriate. Often administrators use the executive summary as a stand-alone document to highlight key findings at meetings, media events, and the like.

Introduction. A two- to three-paragraph introduction is a good way to set the stage for the evaluation report and how the project came to be. In addition, the introduction should contain the overall *purpose* of the evaluation, the *name of the client* or organization for which the report is being written, and both the *project goals* and the *evaluation objectives.*

Methods. In this section the evaluator presents an overview of the different types of tools that were developed, when they were administered, what kinds of data were collected, and the sources for the data.

Body of the Report. The body of the report contains the analyzed data and findings from the evaluation. It is best if you start off each new objective on a new page. First, the evaluation objective should be restated, followed by another short description of what tools were used, what kinds of data were collected, and from whom. Following this, the evaluator will want to report the summarized data in a table or a figure or in bulleted form. Based on this information, the evaluator will then generate an evaluation finding or findings. These evaluation findings are generally an overall theme or summary of the data that are being presented. Additional data that supports the main data and findings can be presented in bullet form under the main table (see Exhibit 1.3).

EXHIBIT 1.3. Overview of Evaluation Objective and Finding

Objective 3: To document stakeholder perceptions of the lessons learned and the strengths of and barriers to the weekend follow-up sessions.

The purpose of this objective was to document stakeholder perceptions of both lessons learned from the experience and the strengths of and barriers to the weekend follow-up sessions. To meet this objective, qualitative data were gathered via either one-to-one interviews or focus groups. Parent perceptions data were provided through open-ended questions on the survey.

Finding: All stakeholders reported that maintaining friendships and becoming motivated to learn and build skills were the strengths of participating in the experience; lack of full participation and inconsistent attendance at follow-up sessions were noted by some to be barriers. Table 3.1 presents these findings by stakeholder category.

(Exhibit 1.3 continued)

Table 3.1. Stakeholder Perceptions of Strengths of and Barriers to Follow-up Sessions

Stakeholder	Strengths	Barriers	Suggestions
Program Director	• Continued friendships, making new friends • Exposure to students from different schools and background • Students continuing to learn and refine skills learned from previous lessons.	• Tutoring sessions occurring at same time • Families moving • Lack of contact information • Transportation • Conflicts with other school or family obligations	See if tutoring could come before or after; better integration
Camp Instructors	• Continued friendships, making new friends • Exposure to students from different schools and background • Students continuing to learn and refine skills learned from previous lessons	• Only 50% of students attending • Month of time between each follow-up session too long • Difficult to keep students on target with learning between sessions • Inconsistency with student attendance, difficult to provide continuity	Linking students together via Internet or Blackboard
Campers	• Able to see friends and stay in touch • Able to learn more about history and storytelling • Able to improve computer skills	• Sessions too short, need to be longer • Not all students attended	• Lengthen sessions • Mandatory attendance
Parents	• Continue learning and growing • Friends	Family or school obligations on same day; sessions were known about in advance so planning could occur	Overall, Saturday mornings a good time

(Exhibit 1.3 continued)

Finding: Camp instructors noted that this experience has benefited their own pedagogy and teaching at the college level, as follows:

- Examination of qualitative data revealed that camp instructors noted several areas in which their work serving as instructors for camp has benefited or changed how they think about or deliver instruction at the college level. More specifically, instructors noted that because of this experience they have tried to do more with interactive activities in their college classroom and have seen how effective such practices are when teaching an adult population.

- Camp instructors reported that this experience has also changed how they instruct others to work with urban at-risk youth. More specifically, instructors have gained this insight: it is important to stress to preservice teachers that when instructing students from these backgrounds they should allow for extra time to start an activity, as it takes these students a little more time to get into the activity.

Finding: Stakeholders noted several areas in which changes could be made to next year's programming in relation to the follow-up sessions:

- To address the issue of low attendance at follow-ups. During the initial greeting of parents at the summer camp, the follow-up sessions will be stressed, as well as their function to support and extend the work and learning that has occurred at summer camp. Parents will be reminded of these sessions at the closing of camp, and perhaps via a notice sent out at the beginning of the school year.

- Offer incentives for students to attend the follow-up sessions. Stakeholders believed that offering some type of incentive to students for completing the follow-up sessions would greatly help to increase the low attendance and to decrease inconsistencies in attendance that occurred with this year's sessions.

- Lengthen the time for sessions. Another area to be addressed is the time constraint with the current three-hour sessions. Stakeholders noted that combining two months of sessions would allow for a half- or quarter-day field trip to a museum or other appropriate educational venue.

- Increase parent involvement. Stakeholders also noted the need for more parent involvement in the follow-up sessions; they believed that field trips could be used as a way to get more parents involved.

Dissemination and Use of Evaluation Findings

It is the role and responsibility of the evaluator to deliver the evaluation report on time. The report should be delivered to the client or agency that has directly commissioned the work to be conducted. In the case of summer-enrichment programs, the client will most likely be an administrator or a project director (or both). In most cases it is the responsibility of the administrator or project director to submit the final evaluation report to the funding agency. Even if an evaluator has established trust and a positive relationship with a particular stakeholder group (such as parents), he or she cannot give the evaluation report to the group without the expressed permission of the client. Once the client has reviewed and made comments to the evaluator, the client will disseminate the report to whichever groups he or she feels should receive it. In some cases the client may wish to have the evaluator present the key findings from the executive summary at an upcoming project meeting and field any questions that stakeholders may have.

The appropriate use of evaluation findings and recommendations are key to a successful evaluation project. Ideally, throughout the process the evaluator has established a professional degree of trust among the stakeholders he or she has been working with. One of the silent roles of the evaluator is to present evaluation findings and recommendations to the client in such a way as to make change occur. The role of the evaluator does not stop with the delivery of the report and recommendations. The evaluator should work with the client to address these issues, and to continue to gather and feed data back to the client until they are resolved.

One way an evaluator can monitor progress toward meeting the recommendations for the project is to build this activity into an evaluation objective. As part of the evaluation of the camp, the evaluation team did just that: they built in a specific objective that focused on the project staff's ability to address limitations or concerns within the project. At the end of the camp all areas of concern had been successfully addressed. Exhibit 1.4 presents this objective.

EXHIBIT 1.4. **Example of Evaluation Objective Focused on Program Modifications**

Objective 5: To document modifications made to programming based on year one program evaluation recommendations

The purpose of this objective was to document any programmatic changes that were conducted in year two that were based on program evaluation recommendations from year one. To complete this objective, a review of the year one follow-up report was conducted. In addition, qualitative data were gathered from stakeholders and data across the entire report were analyzed to determine

(Exhibit 1.4 continued)

whether program refinements had been made and whether they were successful. Finding: In 2004-2005, all recommendations made from year one were addressed and intended outcomes were achieved.

Table 5.1. Status of Prior Recommendations Made to the Summer Camp Follow-Up Sessions

2003-2004 Recommendations	2004-2005 Changes	Results	Status
Increase interest and awareness of follow-up sessions during summer camp 2004.	An emphasis was made by prior campers and staff to increase awareness of follow-up sessions.	There was a 50% increase in total number of campers attending follow-up sessions.	Achieved
Decrease number of sessions, increase length to include trips.	Number of sessions was shortened from six to five total.	Campers attended a full day trip to Boston.	Achieved
Provide field trip opportunities.	• Five Rivers— snowshoeing • Albany— Underground Railroad tour • Boston	Campers realized that learning can take place outside of a classroom environment.	Achieved
Provide an incentive for completing follow-up activities.	Culminating activity was a trip to Boston's aquarium, IMAX, and planetarium.	A total of thirty campers attended the culminating activity.	Achieved

KEY CONCEPTS

Client

Formative evaluation

Summative evaluation

Benchmarks

Program

Internal evaluators

External evaluators

Objective-based approach

Goal-free approach

Expertise-oriented approach

Participant-oriented approach

SUGGESTED READING

Cousins, J. B., & Earl, L. M. (1992). The case for participator evaluation. *Education Evaluation and Policy Analysis*, *14*(4), 397–418.

MacNeil, C. (2002). Evaluator as steward of citizen deliberation. *American Journal of Evaluation*, *23*(1), 45–54.

Patton, M. Q. (2002). *Qualitative research and evaluation methods*. Thousand Oaks, CA: Sage.

PART

2

CASE STUDIES

CHAPTER

2

IMPROVING STUDENT PERFORMANCE IN MATHEMATICS THROUGH INQUIRY-BASED INSTRUCTION

LEARNING OBJECTIVES

After reading this case study you should be able to

1. Note the key differences between an external and internal evaluator and list several benefits and challenges for each

2. Describe the key components of the request for proposal (RFP) process and the role the evaluator plays in all of this

3. Describe the purpose of a needs assessment and how information gathered through this process is sometimes utilized

4. Understand an evaluation matrix and be able to develop one for an evaluation project

5. Understand the use of pre-post surveys, observations, and semistructured interviews

THE EVALUATOR

While finishing his coursework in program evaluation, graduate student Thomas Sanders decided to try his hand at consulting. He had heard of former graduate students setting up evaluation consultancy practices, and he wanted to see for himself if he could do the same.

One of the first challenges Thomas had to address was to find *clients*— people, groups, agencies that needed to hire him and his evaluation services. Thomas began by trying to generate a list of potential clients, but he had difficulty coming up with names to contact. His graduate work had provided him with a wide variety of real-world experience, evaluating projects in the local community. In addition, he had always worked on evaluation projects using a team approach with other graduate students and a faculty advisor from the university, setting up the projects and overseeing them. In actuality, he had never before conducted an evaluation on his own. In fact, Thomas had to admit that the very thought of running an evaluation project solo was both exciting and a little intimidating, to say the least.

Unsure where to start, Thomas decided to seek the guidance of a faculty member in school administration. He knew this faculty member had both program evaluation experience and close contacts with many of the area's public school administrators. So he made an appointment with the faculty member and a week later met him at his office. Thomas explained the kinds of projects he was interested in working on with clients. The faculty member knew that Thomas was a competent student and certainly passionate about evaluation, so he had no problem with giving Thomas a list of names to start contacting. The faculty member strongly encouraged Thomas to pursue school cooperative bureaus. These regional bureaus were located around the state and provided a range of services to the school districts in their regions. The faculty member told Thomas that in his experience these bureaus often were looking to hire evaluators as consultants to work on various grant-funded projects.

Taking the faculty member's advice, and eager to get started, Thomas sent a letter of introduction to all sixteen regional boards across the state. He believed that by doing such a mass mailing he would get at least a couple of bureaus interested in his evaluation services.

A week after sending out his mailing, Thomas received a phone call from one of the bureau directors. The director told Thomas that his letter had been perfectly timed. They had recently received a math initiative grant from the state to address low student performance at the middle school level. She explained that their bureau had thirteen districts in their region that were eligible to participate in the project and, as part of the grant requirement, had to hire an *external evaluator* to evaluate and monitor the project's progress. As they were going to have a kickoff meeting the following week, she suggested that she e-mail the *project narrative* to Thomas for him to review and see if he was interested in coming on board with the project. In addition, she asked that, following the review of the project, he draft a proposal for an *evaluation plan* that he would do based on the project narrative, which he could present to the thirteen school district superintendents at the upcoming meeting.

Following their conversation, the director e-mailed Thomas, thanking him for his time and attaching a detailed narrative of the project and the state's original *request for proposal (RFP)*.

Although not all RFPs are the same, all well-structured RFPs have some common elements, listed here with a brief description of each:

- *Need for the project:* In this section, applicants are required to provide both a narrative and evidence as to why the project is needed. For education-based projects, this is typically done through an analysis of student performance scores on state exams at either the district or the school level. Here is where the *grant writer* demonstrates through the use of data that the students are not performing to a certain *benchmark,* standard, or preestablished criteria.

- *Project narrative:* The project narrative (which the director e-mailed Thomas for review) is the document in which the grant writer, in as much detail as possible, describes the *stakeholders* for whom the proposed project will be structured and implemented in the intended setting and gives an overview of the types of activities the project would provide, overall goals of the project, and project staff and their related responsibilities. This generally includes an overview of the types of activities the project would provide, overall goals of the project, and project staff and their related responsibilities.

- *Evaluation Plan:* The evaluation plan is another key section of any successful proposal. This section is generally undertaken by the program evaluator, who will serve as a nonbiased external evaluator for the project if it is funded. In as much detail as possible, the evaluation plan lays outs the project goals and objectives and discusses methodologies and timelines for data collection and reporting of findings to the appropriate groups.

- *Budget Narrative:* This narrative is a summary description of the project's overall budget and the various allocations to specific budgetary categories.

- *Budget:* The budget summary provides a broad description of the budget; the actual budget provides much more detailed line items for the project. In some cases, budget categories (for example, equipment) may be limited to a certain amount of money. Such restrictions would be indicated in the RFP.

BOX 2.1. The RFP Process

No matter what area of program evaluation you pursue, the RFP process (depicted in Figure 2.1) is one with which professional evaluators, particularly those who serve as external evaluators, become very familiar. This process may vary a little from setting to setting, but in general the main components are similar to those presented in the figure. The RFP process begins with a *funding agency* (step A in Figure 2.1) or a related group who develops an RFP to fund a certain type or series of projects. Funding agencies come in many shapes and sizes. They include state agencies, such as the state's department of public health or education; federal agencies such as the National Science Foundation or the U.S. Department of Agriculture; and private foundations and not-for-profit organizations.

The purpose of the RFP is to invite eligible applicants to apply for funding for a project. For example, the state may have monies to fund after-school programming and therefore develops an RFP inviting school districts in that state to apply. However, not all school districts may be eligible. Determining eligibility will vary depending on the RFP and the funding agency's goals for the initiative. In education, typically eligible schools are those who have consistently shown low student performance on state standardized measures. These measures have been, for the most part, criterion- or standards-based and have predominately focused on English Language Arts (ELA) and mathematics. These low-performing schools are placed on the School in Need of Improvement (SINI) list by their state's department of education. Although being on the list doesn't necessarily guarantee that these districts will receive funding through an RFP, it does provide a wider range of opportunities for districts to obtain additional funding.

Despite the fact that an RFP is used to standardize the process, not all projects funded under the RFP will look exactly the same. Because the RFP provides broad criteria, two school districts could both receive funding and go about implementing two programs that have the same intended goals and objectives but look very different. As shown in step B of Figure 2.1, once the RFP has been created it is posted or disseminated through various channels to those who are eligible to apply. In most cases, particularly with state and federal agencies, RFPs are usually posted on the agency's main website. Most (but not all) RFPs have a deadline by which eligible groups must apply. Eligible applicants obtain the RFP and, using it as a guide, create a project or program that meets the goals set forth by the funding agency. This is the point at which these potential sites would contract with an external evaluator to work on writing an evaluation section of the grant proposal.

As shown in step C, once the RFP has been completed, the eligible groups submit their proposals to the funding agency and wait to see who will receive the awards. *Award* is the common term for acceptance of a group's application as a viable project by the funding agency. A point-based scoring system or rubric is generally used by funders to consistently score or judge each applicant. The number of awards is typically determined by the total amount of funding available for the project.

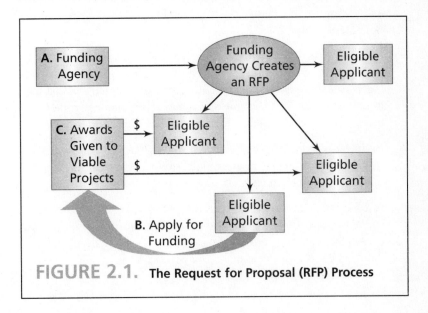

FIGURE 2.1. The Request for Proposal (RFP) Process

THE PROGRAM

The overall purpose of the math program that Thomas was to evaluate was to provide high-quality *professional development* or training to teachers and administrators. Prior to applying for the grant, the bureau director had conducted a needs assessment of the thirteen eligible districts. *Needs assessment* is a general term used for collection of data from a setting to determine which issues are the most important and thus need to be addressed first. In some educational settings this is referred to as "identifying the gap." Multiple methods may be used to collect needs assessment data; however, surveys are probably the most common method used for this purpose.

Through conducting her needs assessment, the director discovered the following:

- Teachers were "unsure" and "not confident" in what they perceived inquiry-based instruction to be.

- School principals and some district superintendents also reported that they were not completely clear on what constituted a "good" inquiry-based lesson.

- In addition, some administrators reported that they often used "inquiry-based learning" as a buzzword and that they lacked the confidence to walk in and conduct an observation of a teacher's lesson and to determine whether it was a "quality" inquiry-based instructional lesson or not.

- Both teachers and administrators also reported that they were uncertain as to whether they often purchased curriculum materials (such as textbooks, programs) that were inquiry-based and that they often had to rely on the publisher's sales representative, rather than being able to review them and make the decision on their own.

- Both teachers and administrators realized that little inquiry-based instruction was occurring in the middle school classrooms, particularly in the area of mathematics.

- And both teachers and administrators believed that it was because students were not being exposed to this type of instruction in math classes that they had performed particularly poorly on problem-based items on the fourth-grade math assessment. An item analysis of the previous fourth-grade math assessment had confirmed this.

Pleased at the wealth of information she had discovered, the director realized that there was a lot of work to be done if the bureau was ever to help these districts raise their math scores. She also believed that professional development would be best suited to address many of the issues. However, she also realized that offering teachers, administrators, and other related staff technical workshops on inquiry-based instruction was not the solution. She knew from the current research that such professional development trainings, even a well-thought-out series of workshops, typically have little impact and create few changes in how people function or teach. Instead, she needed to come up with a unique structure for the program.

In her opinion, to be successful, to gain buy-in from all vested parties, and to meet its overall intended outcomes, the program had to have the following components:

- High-quality professional development from an outside source (such as experts in the fields of education, inquiry-based learning, mathematics, and classroom instruction).

- Establishment of a steering committee, which would meet six times a year to monitor the progress of the program, review evaluation feedback, and make programmatic decisions based on this data.

- One lead teacher from each of the thirteen middle schools. These lead teachers would serve as liaisons between the steering committee and the middle-level teachers being served by the program.

- Middle school teachers from each of the thirteen schools.

- A math consultant who would rotate across the thirteen schools and provide both group assistance to lead teachers and middle-level teachers as well as in-class support to teachers.

THE EVALUATION PLAN

From his graduate work, Thomas knew that the first step in any successful evaluation is for the evaluator to develop an evaluation plan. As part of that process, Thomas reviewed the project narrative in the RFP, then began to draft his evaluation objectives for the project. In examining the project, Thomas noted that the project appeared to have three main functions or phases:

- Phase one focused on professional development, providing training to the middle school teachers.

- Phase two examined whether—and if so, how—those professional development activities had changed teacher practices in the classroom.

- Phase three examined whether there were any outcomes or results of these new teaching practices in student outcomes (see Figure 2.2).

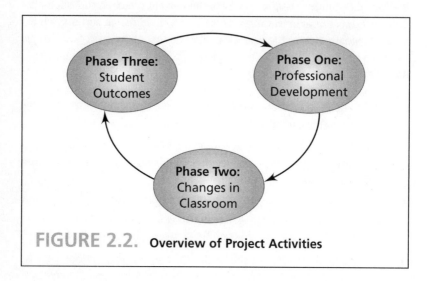

FIGURE 2.2. **Overview of Project Activities**

Based on this information, Thomas created three main evaluation objectives and multiple subobjectives for each main objective. Box 2.2 presents Thomas's evaluation objectives.

BOX 2.2. Thomas's Evaluation Objectives

1. To document the breadth, depth, and quality of the professional development activities.

- Review and document professional development activities and all materials and curriculum associated with the trainings to ensure that the trainings are indeed inquiry-based, student-centered approaches.

- Document teacher baseline perceptions of an inquiry-based, student-centered instruction prior to teachers' participation in the professional development experience.

- Document teacher perceptions of the key issues and challenges in implementing more student-centered practices in their classrooms.
- Document teacher plans for implementing and incorporating inquiry-based instructional practices into the classroom.

2. To document changes in teacher and administrator attitudes, beliefs, and practices in classroom instruction following their participation in the professional development activities.

- Document changes in teachers' instructional practices and determine areas in need of further work and areas for continued professional development.
- Document changes in administrator perceptions of inquiry-based instructional practice.
- Document, where possible, any turnkey training efforts that occurred in the classrooms following the initial professional development trainings.

3. To document changes in student performance.

- Document changes in teacher and staff perceptions about student performance in mathematics.
- Document changes in student performance in classroom and other related activities as they pertain to mathematics.
- Document changes in student performance on the state's math fourth-grade assessment.

Next, Thomas used these evaluation objectives to develop an *evaluation matrix*—a "blueprint." The matrix works to align the evaluation objectives with the tools, their purpose, and the timeline in which they will be administered. Depending on the depth and breadth of the project and its evaluation, these matrixes will vary in their dimensions. Presented in Table 2.1 is the basic template that Thomas used when creating his evaluation matrix.

TABLE 2.1. **Thomas's Evaluation Matrix for the Project**

Evaluation Objectives	Stakeholder Group	Tool, Data, Instrument	Design Timeline

NEXT STEPS

Once the evaluation matrix was completed, Thomas e-mailed it to the director. Two days later, he heard back from her. She had reviewed his matrix and noted that she and her staff were impressed with his proposed evaluation. She also told him that they were interested in hiring him to serve as their external evaluator and invited him to present his plan at the following week's meeting.

For Thomas, the opportunity to serve as an external evaluator on a project to improve mathematical literacy for middle school students in rural school districts was both exciting and personal. He himself had grown up in a rural community and attended a small district school similar to those he was going to be working with on the math project. Having this personal experience, Thomas knew many of the challenges that these rural communities and schools face, such as high poverty rates and limited access to facilities such as libraries and institutions of higher education.

At the meeting, the director presented her ideas for the project and Thomas presented the evaluation plan. Thomas explained how the plan laid out all the essential activities for the evaluation, including "who" the data would be collected from, "how" it would be collected, "when" it would be collected, and the status of the overall activity (that is, completed, not completed, postponed, and so on).

The evaluation plan was well received by those at the meeting. However, one administrator noted that Thomas had not indicated in the plan when such data would be delivered to the committee. In other words, he wanted to know whether the data and findings were formative and therefore would be presented back to the committee at one of the steering committee meetings, or summative and therefore would be reported in the final evaluation report. Thomas thanked the administrator for bringing up the point, and told the committee he would add a column to the plan indicating whether the data were formative or summative. He said he would present the updated evaluation matrix in a couple of months at the next steering committee meeting.

SUMMARY OF EVALUATION ACTIVITIES AND FINDINGS

At the end of August, Thomas, with the help of members from the steering committee, reviewed all documents and materials for the workshops. Although most of these materials met the group's definition of inquiry-based, student-centered instruction, there were a few points that they wanted further emphasized during the workshops. Approximately two hundred middle school teachers attended the six day-long workshops; substitutes were hired to cover their absences. These workshops were held periodically throughout the school year.

During the workshops, Thomas observed the trainings and sat in the various breakout groups with teachers. He participated in the professional development activities that each group was charged with and conducted *semistructured interviews* to gather information from workshop participants. Unlike structured interviews, which follow a list of open-ended questions, semistructured interviews may have several preplanned questions from which the evaluator veers off to ask other, unplanned items. Thomas also administered a teacher survey at the beginning of the first workshop in September and again at the end-of-year workshop in June. Overall, he collected 192 matched, pre-post surveys from approximately 200 teachers. Formative data (such as presurvey data, observations, and interview data) were reported back to the steering committee in several memorandum reports. These data supported many discussions about inquiry-based instruction during the steering committee meetings; in addition, consultants provided committee members with some short presentations on the subject. Lead teachers were also instrumental in returning to their schools and supporting and extending what teachers had been introduced to during the workshops. Lead teachers also met weekly with teams of teachers in their schools and trained other teachers about the promising practices wherever possible. The consultant also worked with teachers across the thirteen districts, both in group settings and one-to-one with teachers in their classrooms. Administrators also filled out post-only surveys at the end of the project.

Overall, the majority of teachers and administrators viewed the project as a success and were, for the most part, pleased with the quality of the professional development in inquiry-based learning and mathematics that they received. The steering committee served as a vital component for the program model, providing a natural loop for formative evaluation data to be presented in a timely manner. Although initially some of the materials for the workshops needed refinement, the professional development was considered to be of high quality and aligned to what teachers and administrators believed was needed at their schools to improve instruction and student performance. Both teachers and administrators reported that they were "not confident" of being able to either instruct using inquiry-based instructional practices or observe others and identify these practices; however, both groups also reported that they believed they were more confident by the end of the project. Teachers also reported that they were trying to implement more inquiry-based instructional practices into their math classes as well as other content areas. Lead teachers supported this finding and in some cases provided Thomas and the steering committee with lesson plans and classroom activities that teachers had developed based on what they had learned from the workshops. Administrators also reported seeing a difference in teachers' instruction that they observed. One administrator created an observational checklist to document inquiry-based practices. He said that he had developed the checklist as a result of what he had learned at the steering committee meetings and from his lead teacher and the consultants. He now used the checklist when observing teachers for tenure. He said staff at his school had "all pulled together and now shared a common vision— one that supported inquiry-based, student-centered practices." The administrator shared this tool with the other administrators at one steering committee meeting and gave a short presentation about how he used the self-developed tool. This presentation fostered further discussion among the administrators about inquiry. Several of these administrators continued to meet on their own to continue this work.

An additional finding, noted in the summative evaluation report, was that in several schools teachers and administrators reported that they had changed their practices for purchasing textbooks, curriculum, and curriculum-related materials. No longer did they rely on curriculum and book publishers' decisions that materials and curriculum were inquiry-based. From this experience they now believed they had the ability to review materials and decide for themselves whether they fit their own definitions of inquiry-based, student-centered instructional practices.

One area that was noted in the model to be "in need of improvement" concerned the consultant who visited the schools to work with lead teachers and groups of teachers and do one-to-one, in-class observations of teachers. Teachers reported that the time allotted for the consultant was not enough to provide proper coverage to all participating districts. Teachers and lead teachers from several districts noted that because of the lack of time, the consultant came to their school only once during the project. Increasing the hours for the consultant or adding another consultant to the model was highly recommended by program participants and documented in Thomas's evaluation report.

In regard to student outcomes, student scores on the fourth-grade state math assessment improved significantly for all thirteen districts on that year's exam. Although there was still plenty of work to be done, this was certainly an encouraging result for these districts. In fact, districts were so encouraged by the initial success of the project that administrators approached the bureau's director hoping to apply to another RFP for mathematics that was due to come out from the state.

LOOKING FORWARD

The director of the bureau was very pleased at the administrators' continued interest in improving mathematic performance and the quality of instruction in their schools. She believed they could credit the program model with the steering committee and a strong evaluation plan that provided formative feedback to committee members and produced a strong buy-in from all parties. The director did not want to stop for even a moment. The momentum and excitement from the district was evident, and she quickly contacted Thomas, wanting to know if he would again serve as their evaluator. This time, however, she told him that they would start developing the program and the evaluation concurrently. Things worked out well for them initially; she was expecting with all the interest the project had generated to have even more success the next time.

About eight months later the state released another RFP for a math and ELA initiative. Several of the administrators contacted Thomas and the bureau director to see if they could set up an initial meeting to start to think about continuing the program that they had started. An initial meeting was set up for the director, Thomas, and the thirteen district administrators.

The morning of the meeting, the director called Thomas. Again they had a positive discussion about how excited everyone was and how all the districts were really coming together to again work on this issue.

"I know the administrators and teachers are really looking forward to this," said the director. "I have worked with these districts for almost twenty-five years, and I have never seen as much positive energy as I have seen with this and the success of our last project."

"It has been great to be a part of," said Thomas, "and I think the next project will be even better."

"I agree," she replied. "Oh, before the meeting let me go onto the state's website to make sure that all thirteen districts are eligible to apply for the new grant."

"OK, good idea," said Thomas.

"I'll see you at the meeting this afternoon."

Thomas hung up and began to gather the papers on his desk for the meeting. Before he could finish packing his bag, the phone rang again. It was the bureau director.

She didn't even give him time to say hello before blurting, "You are not going to believe this."

"What?"

"I just checked the state's web page and none of the thirteen districts is eligible to apply for the new grant."

"What? How can that be?"

"All their scores on the last math assessment went up, so they are no longer on the list. Can you believe it?"

"No, I can't," said Thomas. "I mean, it's a good thing that the scores improved. But a bad thing now that we've gotten everyone all enthusiastic about working to improve math."

"And without the grant we just can't afford to do the extensive professional development that we did before," she said.

"What are we going to do?" asked Thomas.

"I don't know," said the director, "but we only have a couple of hours to figure out how we are going to tell the administrators at our meeting this afternoon."

Thomas hung up the phone. *What was he going to tell these administrators? How would he ever get them on board with another project in the future? How would they ever be able to build such buy-in and enthusiasm again?*

Suddenly he felt sick in his stomach. He didn't know what to do.

Thomas and the director broke the news to the administrators: not a one of them was eligible to apply for the grant. The administrators were disappointed, but also pleased that their districts had shown improvements in math.

FINAL THOUGHTS

Eventually several districts reverted back to being on the SINI list; however, Thomas never worked with any of them again. He finished his degree and took a position at a university three states away. He continued to work with school districts in program evaluation. From his early experience Thomas learned an important lesson that he carried with him for the rest of his career: success on a project may in fact eliminate those hard-working individuals from continued participation.

KEY CONCEPTS

Clients

External evaluator

Project narrative

Evaluation plan

School in Need of Improvement (SINI)

Request for proposals (RFP)

Grant writer

Benchmarks

Funding agency

Award

Needs assessment

Professional development

DISCUSSION QUESTIONS

1. Review Figure 2.1, The RFP Process. Make a list of some of the benefits and challenges you see for schools or other organizations who want to seek such funding to provide additional programming for the people they serve.

2. The situation that Thomas and the bureau director experienced is not uncommon. When projects are a success and project goals are

met, often this means that groups are no longer eligible for funding. Analyze the case again and consider what could be done to continue some elements of this project's design, despite the fact that there is no more funding to hire professional consultants to deliver training and no more stipends for teachers to be trained outside of school.

CLASS ACTIVITIES

1. The feelings of self-doubt that Thomas experienced are not uncommon among new evaluators in training. Reflect on your past evaluation and research projects. Make a list of some key projects you would want to highlight in a conversation with a prospective client. What are some key or unique tools, methods, or practices that you used on these projects? Also, try to think about some of the challenges you had in working on the project. How did you overcome them? What were the results or consequences of your actions?

2. Pretend you too are interested in consulting work in program evaluation. Brainstorm and create a working list of possible clients you might consider approaching. As Thomas did in the case study, do some initial research on the possible clients in your area or field. What are some programs or areas in which you could provide your evaluation consulting skills?

3. In the case study, Thomas demonstrated the importance of a detailed evaluation matrix. Based on the evaluation objectives and subobjectives that Thomas developed, and using the template, develop your own matrix for this project.

SUGGESTED READING

Ding, C., & Navarro, V. (2004). An examination of student mathematic learning in elementary and middles school: A longitudinal look from the US. *Studies in Education Evaluation, 30*(4), 237–253.

Kerney, C. (2005). Inside the mind of a grant reader. *Technology and Learning, 25*(11), 62–66.

Reese, S. (2005). Grant writing 101. *Connecting Education & Careers, 80*(4), 24–27.

Vandegrift, J. A., & Dickey, L. (1993). Improving mathematics and science education in Arizona: Recommendations for the Eisenhower Higher Education Program. ERIC Document No. 365510.

CHAPTER

3

EVALUATION OF A COMMUNITY-BASED MENTOR PROGRAM

LEARNING OBJECTIVE

After reading this case study you should be able to define participatory evaluation and give several examples of how this theory can be applied in practice.

THE EVALUATORS

Evaluator Stephanie Brothers worked for FCA Consulting, a private evaluation firm in the Midwest. Before starting to work at FCA, Stephanie had earned a master's in educational research and had taken several program evaluation courses as electives. One that Stephanie found particularly interesting was a course on *evaluation program theory*. It provided an overview of the various methods and the principles that would guide an evaluator practicing that theory. This course provided Stephanie with some alternative approaches to conducting evaluation, particularly approaches that focused on more of a *participatory evaluation model*.

This evaluation theory focuses on stakeholders or groups developing and collecting their own data and presenting their own findings for the evaluation.

After receiving her master's in educational psychology, Stephanie had applied to private evaluation firms around the country and gone on several interviews. All her interviewers had been very impressed with the amount of course work she had taken geared specifically toward program evaluation—so much so that both firms had immediately offered her a position with their companies.

On her new job at FCA, as Stephanie got to know the people in the firm she had been surprised by their various educational backgrounds and former work experiences. She had assumed that everyone working in a program evaluation firm would have a degree in program evaluation. Several coworkers had advanced degrees in psychology, social work, political science, communication, and technology, and a few were former attorneys, teachers, and school administrators. Although at first Stephanie had been a little concerned that her fellow coworkers did not have the program evaluation background that she had, when working in a team with them she had soon realized that they brought to the table a variety of perspectives and experiences from the field of education and their own work.

In addition to her technical training, working as a middle-level evaluator for FCA provided Stephanie with solid evaluation experience. In September, the company took on a new client: a community-based mentor program for high school students. This program was funded through a three-year grant from the state's department of education and was beginning its second year of the project. However, things had not gone well in the first year of the project. The project director had partnered with an external evaluator, because a rigorous evaluation component that gathered both formative and summative data was required. However, at the end of the first year the program evaluator failed to collect any data on the project and was unable to submit a summative report in order to determine whether the project was meeting its intended goals and objectives. Not filing a project report annually put the project's funding in serious jeopardy. Following this, the program evaluator resigned, and the project director hired FCA to take over the evaluation for the next two years.

For the project, Stephanie was informed that she would serve as principal evaluator and oversee a team of three other employees. Because this was an educational program, team members who had educational backgrounds were chosen. One member of the team had been a school administrator for thirty years, and the other two were trained researchers. Stephanie still could not help but feel a little apprehensive about working with a team whose members were not all formally trained in program evaluation, but she had confidence in herself and felt deep down that they would be able to do a quality job. She also realized how important the evaluation would be, and she was eager to work with the community-based organization.

THE PROGRAM

The purpose of the community-based mentor program was to link volunteers with at-risk high school students. Although the community was considered a small city, it had many of the problems associated with much larger metropolitan areas: many students in the public school district seeking free or reduced lunch, high transient rates among families, high dropout rates among high school students, a high rate of school suspensions, and drug trafficking. In addition, a substantial portion of the school population were not meeting state benchmarks on the state standardized measures, placing the district on the SINI list.

The goal of the program was to provide an after-school structured environment for at-risk high school students through one-to-one mentoring. Mentors were volunteers from the community coming from a wide variety of background, occupations, and educational levels. Each mentor worked with one student. Mentors had their choice of working with mentees at the high school facility after school or at other locations. Many mentors, particularly those who were retired, chose to have their mentees come to their homes. Mentors were required to meet with their mentees at least three times a week for at least one hour per meeting. In some cases, especially for those mentors who were busy professionals and had families of their own, mentoring took place on the weekends.

Although the specifics of the program, such as number and duration of mentor-mentee meetings, were explicitly stated in the program description, Stephanie noticed when she reviewed the program documents that other aspects of the program, such as the type and quality of the activities mentors did with the students, were not specified. It appeared that mentors could pretty much do whatever activities they wanted to with the students they were working with.

THE EVALUATION PLAN

The evaluation team decided that a *mixed-method approach* would be best. The mixed-method approach is a methodology used in research and also in program evaluation, whereby the evaluators collect both quantitative and qualitative data from program participants. Box 3.1 presents the complete list of the program goals; the evaluators would be determining whether these goals were being met.

BOX 3.1. Program Goals

1. To provide each eligible student with access to a community mentor.

2. To work with and provide quality training to mentors.

3. To increase students' academic achievement in school.

4. To decrease incidents of student violence and behavioral problems at school and in the community.

5. To increase the number of at-risk students graduating from high school.

Shortly after their examination of all project documents and materials, Stephanie and the evaluation team had another meeting. They invited Mr. Jonathan Post, the head of the community organization that the school district had partnered with for the mentor project. The evaluators had decided that the purpose of the meeting was to discuss the project and the activities needed to develop the *evaluation capacity* or evaluation tools (a survey, interview protocols, and the like) required to fully evaluate the efforts of the program (see Box 3.2).

BOX 3.2. What Is Evaluation Capacity?

Evaluation capacity is a term commonly used in evaluation. Although it has become a general term, meaning many different things to many different people, typically the term *evaluation capacity* is used by evaluators to describe a process or time period in which evaluation tools are collected and or developed. It is not uncommon for evaluators to use what are referred to as *preestablished tools or instruments*. Preestablished instruments typically have been developed by someone other than the researcher or evaluator. Another characteristic common among preestablished instruments is that they are for the most part standardized. A standardized instrument possesses the following criteria:

> . . . [I]t includes a fixed set of questions or stimuli.

> It is given in a fixed time frame under similar conditions with a fixed set of instructions and identified responses.

> It is created to measure specific outcomes and is subjected to extensive research and development and review.

> And performance on the instrument can be compared to a referent such as a norm group, a standard or criterion, or an individual's own performance [on a norm reference test, a criterion reference test, or a self-referenced test] . . . (Lodico, Spaulding, & Voegtle, 2006, p. 67)

> In most cases, preestablished measures have received extensive testing for reliability and validation during their design and development phases, prior to being marketed and disseminated. Most preestablished measures used in education are developed for professions other than educational researchers or program evaluators. They are used by school administrators, general and special education teachers, school psychologists and counselors, and the like. However, for many projects these tools, the data collected by evaluators, or both may be used to address various evaluation objectives.

Before they met, Stephanie sat down with her team and, using an evaluation matrix, planned some of the activities. Presented in Table 3.1 are the matrix they used and the evaluation activities that they proposed to conduct to meet the program's evaluation objectives.

Through both her course work and her on-the-job training experience, Stephanie had learned that such evaluation plans could be very helpful for both the evaluator and the client. As the team began to lay out

TABLE 3.1. **Template for Planning an Evaluation Project**

Evaluation Objectives	Stakeholder Group	Tools and Instruments or Type of Data	Timeline and Design for Data Collection	Formative or Summative/ Reporting Period	Status

the evaluation activities, Stephanie soon realized that not all her team members believed as much as she did that such detailed planning of the evaluation—which data would be collected when—was important. In fact, one member said, "We are wasting a lot of precious time laying out every detail of this evaluation; we should be out there collecting data— that's what evaluation is all about." Stephanie said she agreed with her team member that evaluation was about collecting data and that they would soon be doing so; however, they also had to realize that producing this plan was not only for them but would serve as a tool or talking points to open up a dialogue with their client.

Grudgingly, her teammates agreed.

On the day of the meeting Mr. Post arrived on time and so did Stephanie's team. After the introductions, Stephanie began by handing out the latest draft of the evaluation matrix to everyone, saying that the team had reviewed the project and come up with the following plan.

"Our next step," Stephanie added, "will be to start to develop our instruments and tools for collecting data. We call this *building evaluation capacity*."

"Tools," said Mr. Post, wrinkling his forehead.

Stephanie knew that often evaluators used language or terms that were unfamiliar to clients. "Surveys, interview protocols—these are tools that evaluators use to collect data," she explained. She pulled a couple of surveys from a previous project and laid them out on the table in front of Mr. Post.

Mr. Post put on his reading glasses and examined the documents. Then he reached into his briefcase, pulled out a stack of papers, and handed them to Stephanie.

"And what is this?" she asked.

"Survey data that we have collected from all the mentors, the students they are working with, and their family members or guardians," said Mr. Post.

"Oh." Stephanie felt her face begin to contort as she flipped through the papers.

"We decided to collect some of the data ourselves to make it easier on whoever stepped in to do the evaluation," said Mr. Post.

Stephanie handed the surveys to the other members of the team, who began to rifle through them. "That's great. I am sure that we can put these to good use."

For the rest of their time together, Stephanie went through the remainder of the evaluation plan and explained it to Mr. Post. She told him their evaluation team would be setting up a *focus group* of mentors to interview. She explained that a focus group was a smaller sample of people, often with similar experiences, who are interviewed in a group setting. She also explained that to ensure that all the program goals were properly addressed, the evaluation team would also be collecting data from the students' schools. She explained that the team would work to get school district permission to obtain access to this sensitive data.

At meeting's end, Mr. Post thanked them for working with the program and said he looked forward to it. The team thanked him for coming, and Stephanie saw Mr. Post out.

After closing the door, Stephanie turned to the other members of her team.

One of them said, "We can't possibly use those surveys and data. Did you look at them? The scales they used make absolutely no sense whatsoever, and the items have nothing to do with evaluating the project's goals and objectives."

"I agree," said another member.

"Circular file," said the third. She pointed to the trash can in the far corner of the room. "Data should only be collected by professional researchers who know what they are doing."

Stephanie could feel her stomach tensing up. "I agree, but what am I supposed to tell Mr. Post?"

"Tell him the truth," said one of the former administrators. "Tell him the data aren't valid or rigorously collected, and we can't use them."

Stephanie joined the others at the conference table and slumped back into her chair. It was true. The data had little if any value. And Stephanie knew they had little use for the data in their evaluation plan. But she also knew that not using it could spell potential disaster for an evaluation project that had already gotten off to a shaky start.

Stephanie opened the folder of completed surveys and started to sort through them again. *Was there anything they could use?* she asked herself. *Anything at all?*

Because of the bad experience that the client and the participant mentors had had with the previous evaluator and the potential harm to the program that such actions might have caused, Stephanie realized that building trust is very important. She convinced the members of her team to use the data collected by the client in their evaluation report. They noted in the report that the survey and data were collected by the participants. Seeing these used in the report and presented at a later meeting built great confidence and trust. The mentors felt that the evaluators were interested in what they had to say about the program. They also realized that their survey didn't exactly address some of the questions or objectives of the evaluation. Recognizing this, Mr. Post worked with Stephanie and her team to design a more rigorous survey, specifically aligned to address some of the projects' evaluation objective and the mentors' needs and questions. The mentors now trusted the evaluation team, and the next time around they allowed the team to collect the data.

SUMMARY OF EVALUATION ACTIVITIES AND FINDINGS

In this case study, Stephanie's past course experience provided her with a perception of program evaluation that was slightly different than that of her colleagues. Despite the fact that the data collected by the client might not have had the rigor that data collected from the evaluators would have had, Stephanie was able to recognize the importance of using the data for the evaluation report. By including the data collected by the client, the evaluation team was able to begin to develop a trust with the client that had been fractured because of past experiences.

FINAL THOUGHTS

Evaluators and clients do not always work closely together. In fact, one aspect of evaluation that evaluators-in-training rarely get exposed to in their course work is how to work with clients. Often evaluators find themselves working with a client who doesn't necessarily see the evaluation process in the same way as the evaluator. Clients may see the evaluator as an intruder, a spy, or a watchdog. Although there may sometimes be some truth in these notions, recognizing these commonly held misperceptions is an important part of being an evaluator, and working with clients through the process of planning the evaluation and collecting and reporting data is a way to bring client and evaluator together.

KEY CONCEPTS

Evaluation program theory

Participatory evaluation model

Mixed-method approach

Evaluation capacity

Focus group

DISCUSSION QUESTIONS

1. As a professional evaluator you will most likely find yourself working with people who have very different backgrounds. One of the wonderful things about program evaluation is that it attracts a wide range of professionals. Take a few minutes and list some of the advantages (and perhaps some disadvantages) you can think of to working on an evaluation team composed of people with such varied experiences. What skills, talents, and past experiences would you be able to bring to the project, and how might you establish an evaluation framework that would work to incorporate both your skills and the skills of members from your team?

2. Unlike what is required for teachers, administrators, school counselors, and school psychologists, there is no official certification by the state or federal government for program evaluators. In essence, anyone can call himself a program evaluator and practice this craft.

Do you think there should be a certification for program evaluators? Why or why not? Note your position and list a few comments for a class discussion that supports your belief on the subject.

3. Read the article in the Suggested Reading that pertains specifically to certification for program evaluators. After reading them, reflect on these pieces. Did anything in them change your opinion about the issues? If so, please be prepared in class to discuss why.

CLASS ACTIVITIES

1. Conduct a literature search on participatory evaluation. You may also want to read the Suggested Reading items that pertain to this. Based on your reading, what should Stephanie do with the data that the client has collected?

2. It is never too early to start preparing for the interview process. Whether you have already been on a job interview for a program evaluation position or not, make a list of the different things you might bring to an interview. These might include past experiences in which you have performed job-related activities that might be valuable to an employer (such as data entry).

3. Surf the web and visit several different colleges and universities and review the different courses that make up their program evaluation degrees.

4. Surf the web and look at newspapers and other media for program evaluation positions. Keep a running list of the different skills that these positions require. Have a discussion in class about where these particular skills are obtained for evaluators-in-training.

SUGGESTED READING

Altschuld, J. W. (1999). The case for a voluntary system for credentialing evaluators. *American Journal of Evaluation, 20*(3), 507–517.

Cousins, J. B., & Whitmore, E. (1998). Framing participatory evaluation. *New Directions for Evaluation, 80*, 5–23.

Jones, S. C., & Worthen, B. R. (1999). AEA members' opinions concerning evaluator certification. *American Journal of Evaluation, 20*(3), 495–506.

King, J. A. (1998). Making sense of participatory evaluation practice. *New Directions for Evaluation, 80*, 57–67.

CHAPTER

4

TEACHER CANDIDATES INTEGRATING TECHNOLOGY INTO THEIR STUDENT TEACHING EXPERIENCE

LEARNING OBJECTIVES

After reading this case study you should

1. Have a better understanding about how to collect and analyze alternative types of data when conducting an evaluation

2. Have a better understanding of how program evaluators create self-developed "tools" in certain situations

3. Have a better understanding of portfolios, how they are used in education as both an instructional and an assessments tool, and some of the noted benefits and challenges with their use

4. Have a more in-depth understanding of some of the various challenges evaluators often face in collecting data, particularly alternative or nontraditional forms of data

THE EVALUATORS

Jason Simpson and Daphne Stevenson were two professional evaluators who had worked in program evaluation in both higher education settings and the areas of teacher candidate programs and portfolios. They were very familiar with the different methods used by colleges and universities to train teacher candidates for the classroom.

THE PROGRAM

Jason and Daphne were evaluating a three-year program conducted by a local university. The university is a major teacher training institute, training approximately one-third of the state's teachers. As part of this new initiative, the university wanted to infuse technology and *technology integration* into their teacher education courses. One of the university's program goals was to increase the exposure to technology that teacher-candidates were getting in their course work, in hopes that this experience would translate into teacher-candidates' increased use of technology in their field placements and student teaching. As part of this effort, the university hoped that through this technology-rich experience they would produce teachers who could integrate technology into their classrooms and therefore be more effective. In addition, the university hoped that teacher-candidates' access to technology would in turn make an impact on the host teachers who supervised these teacher candidates in their field placements and student-teacher settings. To make this initiative possible, the university purchased (through a grant) laptop computers, LCD projectors, digital cameras, and software. As part of their course work, teacher candidates were supposed to check out this equipment (much as they would check out books from a library) and bring it into their student-teaching settings.

THE EVALUATION PLAN

For this particular project the evaluation was underpinned with several objectives, presented in Box 4.1.

BOX 4.1. Evaluation Objectives

1. To document, wherever possible, an increase in knowledge and use of and access to technology for university faculty in the teacher-candidate program

2. To document, wherever possible, an increase in knowledge and use of and access to technology for teacher-candidates enrolled in the university's teacher education program

3. To document an increase in the use and types of technology teacher-candidates are introducing into their field placements and student-teaching settings

4. To document the impact of increased access to technology for teacher candidates in their field placements and student-teacher settings

Jason and Daphne met with the project director to discuss the evaluation. The project director handed out the evaluation objectives to them for the discussion.

"As you can see," said the director, "we have four main evaluation objectives that are guiding our project."

Jason and Daphne reviewed the document and began to take down some notes.

"Now, we have an internal evaluator who has been conducting most of our evaluation for us," said the director. "But according to our grant funder, we also need to hire an external evaluator to conduct some of the evaluation as well."

"We have worked with many internal evaluators before," said Jason.

"Wonderful," said the director. "We would like you to focus on evaluations objectives three and four, mainly three."

Daphne and Jason nodded and reread the last two objectives.

Daphne said, "For objective three, to document the use and types of technology, we will probably want to get a list of the host teachers and meet with them and perhaps interview them—"

"We might even want to create a survey as well and give that to all the host teachers, too," added Jason.

"Well . . ." said the project director. "That might be a problem."

"Why?" both Daphne and Jason said at the same time.

"Well, you have to realize the very important role the host teachers play here in our teacher education program at the university. We rely on them tremendously to have our teacher candidates come into their classrooms for fifteen weeks and do their student teaching . . ."

"We understand," said Daphne. "Both Jason and I have worked in higher education and have conducted evaluations in high ed."

"So you know how vital our host teachers are?"

"Yes, we certainly do."

"Good," said the director. She paused for a moment, then said, "Well, the person at the university who oversees the whole student-teacher component is very concerned that the evaluation of our technology project and all the data collection that will have to be done will become too much of an inconvenience for our host teachers—and we wouldn't want to lose any of them."

"I see," said Jason. "So what does this mean in terms of conducting the evaluation?"

"Well, it means that you won't be able to access the student teaching sites and interview or survey the host teachers."

"What about the teacher candidates? Can we interview them?" asked Daphne.

"Yes, you may," said the director. "However, some of the students have graduated and others have already left for the summer."

Jason asked, "Might we be able to get some contact information for them at home, in case we want to interview them over the phone?"

"We might be able to," said the director. "I would have to ask the dean to see if there are any legal issues regarding the confidentiality of the contact information."

"Are there any other data that would help us evaluate the teacher candidates' experience and how they went about using technology in their student teaching settings and the types of technology they used?" Daphne asked. She hadn't expected the evaluation to take such a turn.

"Not unless their teacher-candidate portfolios would help."

"Teacher-candidate portfolios?" Again they both responded in unison.

The project director went on to explain that during the grant project each teacher candidate had to develop a candidate portfolio and maintain that portfolio throughout the program (see Box 4.2). As part of the portfolio the candidates had to reflect on their student teaching experiences and to show artifacts or documents that supported their ability to meet the twelve competencies required by the program.

BOX 3.2. Overview of Portfolios in Education and Teacher Training

Portfolios have been a cornerstone in education, particularly over the course of the last several decades (Spaulding & Straut, 2006). During the late 1980s and early 1990s, portfolios played a pivotal role in the authentic assessment movement (Wiggins, 1992 and 1998). In addition, studies have examined portfolios for their effects on students' learning in a wide variety of content areas, such as science (Roth, 1994), as well as math, social studies, and literacy. Although a substantial portion of the literature on portfolios has focused on their use for instruction and assessment of student learning, there is also a main thrust in the literature whereby portfolios are used for the training of *teacher candidates*. An examination of the literature on portfolios reveals that much of the work focuses specifically on the use of teacher-candidate portfolios—a traditional cornerstone in the area of teacher preparation programs (Barton & Collins, 1997; Klecker, 2000; Morgan, 1999; Shannon & Boll, 1996). In this context portfolios have played a variety of roles, from assisting new prospective teachers in obtaining employment to serving as one of the main assessment tools for determining program completion and student readiness for graduation (Morgan).

With the increased emphasis now being placed on technology and integration of technology into classroom instruction, portfolios used in teacher preparation programs have also begun to use technology. A review of literature on electronic portfolios, however, found much of the research in this area to be opinion-based rather than empirical. Advocates of the e-portfolio note many benefits from their use from increased creativity for their creators to increased "interactivity" among those stakeholders involved in teacher preparation practices. These stakeholders consist of the teacher candidate, faculty from the teacher education program, and host teacher from the field placement experience (Spaulding, Straut, Wright, & Cakar, 2006).

Using portfolios as a collection of artifacts to demonstrate competencies for teacher candidates has been a longstanding tradition with many of this country's finest teacher preparation institutions. In more recent times, however, these portfolios and the processes associated with them have come under increased scrutiny as the institutions of higher education have worked to incorporate them.

"Can I see one of these portfolios?" Jason asked.

"Certainly." The director turned on a nearby computer, typed a few words on the keyboard, then said, "This is a senior who just graduated from the program."

"They are electronic portfolios?" asked Daphne.

"Yes, another requirement of the program is that all teacher candidates demonstrate that they can create an e-portfolio."

The director clicked on a few links and began to move through the student's portfolio.

"Have you always had portfolios for your teacher-candidate program?"

"Yes; we used to have paper portfolios, but as part of our technology grant project we moved the system to e-portfolios. It allows the faculty to review the students' portfolios much more easily and provide feedback as the students are working on assembling the portfolio."

The director kept scrolling through the e-portfolio.

Daphne and Jason could easily see that the e-portfolio had lots of examples and artifacts showing different ways the teacher candidates had worked to integrate technology into their field placements.

"How many e-portfolios do you have?" asked Jason.

The project director thought for a few moments. "Over the course of the last three years of the project, I would say we have about three hundred portfolios."

"Three hundred?" said Daphne.

"Yes, I would say so, give or take a few."

Daphne looked at Jason with an overwhelmed expression.

"Is it enough data?" asked the director.

"Oh, it's more than enough data, I would think," Daphne finally said with a smile. "But how are we going to go about analyzing it all? That's the real question."

Daphne and Jason found that the portfolios became a rich source of data for evaluation objectives three and four. As they began to review the portfolios, they saw patterns emerging among the artifacts the teacher candidates had included to document their technology efficiency. Daphne and Jason began a running list of these patterns and eventually created a checklist of possible ways in which student-teachers integrated technology into their student-teaching classrooms. Exhibit 4.1 presents the checklist that they developed.

EXHIBIT 4.1. Technology Use and Integration Checklist for Portfolio Analysis

Candidate shows evidence of being able to use technology.

For example, candidate

• Has created an e-portfolio using PowerPoint

• Has digital or video artifacts in portfolio; these may be digital pictures of the field placement classroom or students studying or working together

Note: These are not necessarily examples in which the candidate or his or her students are using technology.

Candidate shows evidence of integrating technology into instruction for *didactic teaching* purposes. An example of this is the candidate introducing PowerPoint to the setting and delivering direct instruction of a lesson through the use of this technology.

Candidate shows evidence of integrating technology into instruction for *inquiry-based teaching* or for student-collaborative purposes, whereby students are asking questions and using technology to collect data to answer them; for example, having students conduct "research."

Candidate shows integration of technology in field placement classroom and describes how technology or technology integration was used to address *a particular issue or problem in the school or classroom as it relates to instruction.*

Candidate shows integration of *assistive technology* in field placement classrooms to meet students' special learning needs.

Candidate shows evidence of a product that he or she has developed using technology. This may be an entirely new lesson that integrates the use of technology. In this situation students (not the instructor) are using the technology.

Candidate shows evidence of working collaboratively with *host* teacher to integrate technology into the field placement classroom

Candidate shows evidence of working collaboratively with *other staff,* such as technology support personnel or administrator to address technology issues or integrate technology into the field placement classroom.

Candidate shows evidence of student work that uses technology and *assesses* the student work to determine whether the student has reached the learning objectives.

Candidate shows evidence of student work that uses technology and assesses the student work to determine whether the student has reached the learning objectives. If the student has not, then candidate provides evidence that supports *refinement for instructional practices* or a change of the use of technology.

SUMMARY OF EVALUATION ACTIVITIES AND FINDINGS

Daphne and Jason's evaluation plan was a success. In analyzing the portfolios using the checklist they discovered 95 percent of the teacher candidates provided artifacts or examples in their portfolios of each of the categories on the technology checklist. The evaluators presented this information back to the client. As part of their presentation the evaluation team decided to use examples of the teacher candidates' work to support their findings. The clients were pleased with both the presentation and the wide variety of technology usage that teacher candidates were able to demonstrate in their portfolios. With both the work that the university's internal evaluator had conducted and Daphne and Jason's contribution, the program director was able to provide sufficient evidence back to the funder to show that the program had successfully met all of its evaluation objectives.

FINAL THOUGHTS

Many times, evaluators like Daphne and Jason find themselves in situations where they cannot always collect the data that they would prefer to collect. In such situations, evaluators often have to step back and think about other data they can collect using alternative approaches. In this case study, Daphne and Jason respected the wishes of the project director not to overtax host teachers with an array of surveys and interviews, but instead examined the setting and found that the teacher candidates' portfolios provided a wealth of information to meet their evaluation objectives.

KEY CONCEPTS

Portfolios

Teacher candidates

Technology integration

DISCUSSION QUESTIONS

1. Sometimes evaluators are faced with challenges in collecting the kinds of data and the quality and quantity of data that they would ideally like. In this case, Daphne and Jason are faced with the fact

that they are not going to have access to the host teachers. Review the case again and be prepared to enter into a discussion about how you would go about dealing with this dilemma if you were the evaluator.

2. In examining the portfolios Daphne and Jason are looking for different ways that teacher candidates have documented integrating technology into their student-teaching classrooms. Are there any other types of analyses that you can think of for analyzing the portfolios? If so, be prepared to share them in a class discussion.

CLASS ACTIVITIES

1. Contrary to what many may think, not all work in program evaluation in education focuses directly on programs in public school, teacher instruction, and student learning and behavioral outcomes. The ways in which we train our teachers of tomorrow to use technology or a host of other instructional approaches are also commonly examined, as in the program in this case study. Therefore, in your role as an evaluator who will one day work in the field of education, it is important that you understand fundamentally how teacher programs are designed. Take a look at three or four of your local colleges' and universities' education programs on the web. Note some of the commonalities you see across programs. What are some differences? Be sure to note the number of credits that constitute each program and the different programs available: childhood education, secondary education, special education, and so on. Also be sure to pay particular attention to the different field placements and student teaching opportunities that each of these institutions provides. Be prepared to present your findings in class and have a discussion with other class members about how teachers are trained for the classroom.

2. Find a teacher who uses technology in his or her classroom. Set up a time to go in and conduct several observations of the teacher and the class using the technology observation checklist developed by Jason and Daphne. Did the observational protocol hold true? Were there ways in which the teacher integrated technology that were picked up by the protocol? Were there any ways in which the teacher integrated technology that were not on the protocol? Be ready to present your observations and findings in class.

SUGGESTED READING

Mouza, C. (2002–2003). Learning to teach with new technology: Implications for professional development. *Journal of Research on Technology in Education, 35*(2), 272–289.

Page, M. S. (2002). Technology-enriched classrooms: Effects on students of low socioeconomic status. *Journal of Research on Technology in Education, 34*(4), 389–409.

CHAPTER

5

EVALUATION OF A PROFESSIONAL DEVELOPMENT TECHNOLOGY PROJECT IN A LOW-PERFORMING SCHOOL DISTRICT

LEARNING OBJECTIVES

After reading this case study, you should be able to

1. Understand benchmarking and be able to generate benchmarks for an evaluation project

2. Define what a logic model does and give its main components

3. Discuss some of the benefits of collecting evaluation data while the project is occurring and some of the challenges in performing an evaluation after a project has ended

THE EVALUATOR

Samantha Brown had worked for the Johnstown City School District for ten years. Like many of the school staff, Samantha—or "Miss Sam," as everyone at the school calls her—wore many hats. Her official title was director of special projects. One of her main responsibilities was to pursue and oversee special projects that are outside of the district's normal curriculum and funding. She spent most of her time trying to obtain externally grant-funded projects for the district. In most cases, she pursued RFPs from the state and federal governments and other related funding agencies, and she wrote grants in hopes of being awarded these additional monies to support such initiatives.

Although Sam did not have a degree in program evaluation or grant writing, she did have an undergraduate degree in communication and a master's in English. Sam had strong communication and writing skills. One summer she completed grant writing workshops at the local university, and she had also attended grant writing and program planning conferences. Accordingly, although Sam did not have formal training in program evaluation, she was familiar with it because of her grant writing work.

THE PROGRAM

The district had focused significant time and energy on the area of technology, particularly with regard to increasing teachers' ability to successfully integrate technology into their classrooms. In fact, the district had spent the last three years developing the technology infrastructure at their three elementary schools, two middle schools, and high school. Although it had been very costly, the state technology grants that they had managed to acquire provided them with the monies to wire all their school buildings for the Internet. In addition, the district had been able to build three computer labs at the high school, a computer lab and cart at each of the middle schools, and two mobile computer labs at each of the three elementary schools. The mobile labs consisted of carts holding twenty wireless laptop computers, a teacher computer, an LCD projector, and a DVD player.

Along with providing the hardware and software to the buildings, each year the district had also used the grant monies to hire several consultants to provide a variety of professional development workshops for their teachers and other appropriate staff members. Because of the wide range of computer abilities, workshops ranged from basic computer skills and knowledge to more advanced computer skills, such as integrating technology into teachers' instructional practices and using technology to meet all students' learning needs.

As part of this process, the district had also made evaluation of the project part of the job responsibilities for the district's technology coordinator. However, during the three years of the technology project, there had been three different technology coordinators. Currently the position remained vacant.

Sam's Evaluation Assignment

One day Sam received a call from the superintendent. He informed Sam that although he was very pleased at what the technology project had done for the district, there had been little in the way of program evaluation for the project. In fact, he had just received a phone call from the technology coordinator at the state department of education, telling him that the program was supposed to have an annual program evaluation and that the state had never received an evaluation report during the project's three years. The coordinator had informed the superintendent that the Johnstown School District would be ineligible to apply for future RFPs in technology if an evaluation report that encompassed the last three years' work was not submitted within thirty days.

The superintendent asked Sam to design and carry out an evaluation for the district's technology program within the deadline placed on them by the state. Sam told the superintendent that she would try her best. He thanked Sam for all her hard work in securing the external funds, but reminded her that if the district didn't meet this challenge, the district as a whole would not be able to continue with its technology initiative.

Unsure where to start, Sam decided that her first step would be to gather all the data that the previous technology coordinators had collected. Next she would review those data, compare them to the main goals of the grant, and then determine what additional data she would need to write the project's summative evaluation report.

Sam was given access to the office of the former technology coordinator. Going through the file cabinets, she was pleased to come across a large binder marked "DATA FOR TECHNOLOGY GRANT."

Things are looking up, Sam told herself. *We might make the state's deadline after all.*

But her hopes were quickly dashed: when she opened the binder, it was empty.

THE EVALUATION PLAN

Later, back in her office, Sam opened her files for the project and found three documents. The first was a listing of the intended *benchmarks* the district had originally proposed to meet. Benchmarks are developed to help gauge whether the program, incentive, or activity is producing the results or outcomes deemed necessary by a group. When performance is being examined, benchmarks are generally put in place to allow for comparisons across groups (Mathison, 2005). Table 5.1 presents the benchmarks for Sam's evaluation assignment.

TABLE 5.1. The District's Technology Benchmarks

Benchmark 1	100% of students have access to technology (such as computers) on a daily basis.
Benchmark 2	100% of students have a basic understanding of computer functions and applications.
Benchmark 3	100% of students have the opportunity to participate in technology-rich learning environments (such as the classroom) where technology is being used to both deliver and drive instruction.
Benchmark 4	100% of students have the opportunity to participate in student-centered or -directed projects and guide their own learning.
Benchmark 5	100% of students have the skills and opportunity to work with and train other students in using technology.
Benchmark 6	100% of students are able to develop technology-rich activities, lessons, and products and can demonstrate how these components meet the state's learning standards.

In addition, Sam came across a *logic model* that she and others had created when writing the initial grant. A logic model is an organizer used by evaluators to think about, collect, and manage different kinds of data. Table 5.2 presents the logic model Sam found.

TABLE 5.2. **Overview of Logic Model Guiding the Project Evaluation**

Logic Model Component	Operational Definitions
Activities	This first component of the logic model is to document activities and events that occur as part of the project, including but not limited to workshops, trainings, meetings, field trips, and so on. The purpose of this component is not to focus on outcomes of the activity but to simply document the activity itself, its purpose, and whether the participants believed the activity met its intended goals and objectives.
Outputs of Activities	Although outputs of activities are certainly related to the activities themselves, the purpose of this component is to document outputs or changes that have occurred as a result of participants' engagement in such activities. Outputs tend not to be direct changes in one's action (for example, changes in teaching practices), but rather changes in one's thinking, beliefs, or opinions, particularly in relation to the project. Here's an output example: after teachers attend a workshop on working with students from at-risk populations, they realize that (1) all students can, indeed, learn; and (2) they as teachers may have been implementing teaching strategies that were inconsistent with this new belief.
Intermediate Outcomes	This component focuses on documenting changes in practice. As in the previous example, the instructor goes back to the classroom and changes instructional practices to match these new beliefs. Intermediate outcomes can also be changes in student behavior and student learning. These are not changes on standardized test scores or state assessments, but changes in student ability in the classroom. Examples include increases in student homework completed, greater student interest in subject areas, and higher student scores on quizzes and unit tests.
End Outcomes	Commonly referred to as *hard outcomes,* these typically are changes in student performance on a standardized measure (such as a state or standardized assessment). During the evaluation process, end outcomes typically take four to six years from the project implementation to emerge.

BOX 5.1. Overview of Logic Models

Increasingly popular among program evaluators in recent times, the idea of using logic models has been around since its introduction in the 1960s with the work of Suchman and others (as cited in Rogers, 2005). Although logic models are typically displayed using diagrams or flowcharts, Rogers notes that they can also be portrayed through the use of narratives. More important, program evaluators should recognize that logic models can be developed either before program implementation or after completion of activities—the latter in an *ex post facto* (after-the-fact) evaluation.

According to Rogers, critics of logic models noted that those focusing on certain processes and outcomes may in fact limit the evaluator's ability to locate other unanticipated points of the program and outcomes. In addition, logic models are not exclusively designed by evaluators. In fact, many evaluators take full advantage of designing logic models through working collaboratively with their clients and or stakeholders.

Because of time constraints, Sam realized that collecting data from multiple sources (such as surveys, interviews, observations, document analyses) was not going to be possible. She decided that a well-designed survey administered to all teachers in the district would be the only methodology that would collect such a wide range of data in a timely fashion. But would she be able to develop a survey instrument that would allow her to capture all the data necessary to tie back and meet the various sections of the logic model?

Using the logic model as her guide, Sam was able to develop a survey that collected ex post facto data for each of the model's components. She was then able to take the data for the logic model and address each of the technology benchmarks developed prior to project implementation.

Overall, despite the lack of annual evaluation, it appeared that the district met most of the benchmarks. The evaluation also revealed that most teachers and staff were comfortable with basic computer skills and wanted to work on more specific aspects of integrating technology into their classrooms. In addition, teachers also wanted more professional development in using assistive technology to meet the learning needs not only of students with special needs but also of all the learners in their buildings.

When the next technology RFP came out from the state department of education, Sam went to work, writing a grant that would help the district to purchase additional computers for the buildings and provide professional development for assistive technology. The district was awarded $400,000 for three years to heighten the use of technology in order to decrease the gap in performance on state assessments between general education and special education students. In her grant proposal, Sam made sure to state that the district would hire an external evaluator to perform the evaluation on an annual basis.

SUMMARY OF EVALUATION ACTIVITIES AND FINDINGS

Many times people in certain positions find themselves having to conduct program evaluation. As in Sam's case, often they find that past evaluations of the program have been less than ideal. In this case, however, Sam was able to use her past experience and background in program evaluation. By fully examining the situation and understanding the program goals and evaluation objectives, she was able to develop an evaluation plan that could be executed quickly and efficiently to obtain the data required by the funding agencies. Other, less experienced evaluators might not have been so successful if they tried to implement an evaluation plan that did not take into consideration the constraints under which the data collection was taking place.

FINAL THOUGHTS

In the end Sam was able to take a bad situation and, using her knowledge of research and program evaluation methods, salvage the program and gain future funding. From this experience Sam learned a lot about herself as an evaluator and the importance of program evaluation in relation to continued funding of a program. When working with programs after that, Sam was always keenly aware to make sure the program evaluator was collecting data throughout the course of the project, and she required her evaluators to submit quarterly or biannual reports that provided formative data to the project as well as ensured that the necessary data were getting collected. Sam made certain there would never again be another empty folder waiting for her.

KEY CONCEPTS

Benchmarks

Logic models

Ex post facto evaluation

 ## DISCUSSION QUESTIONS

1. In examining the program's structure, what do you think might be some initial benefits of the mobile cart labs over the traditional computer labs?

2. Sam has found herself in quite a predicament in relying on the district's technology coordinator to serve as the project's main internal evaluator. Knowing what you know about the role and responsibilities of an external evaluator compared with an internal evaluator, discuss some of the pros and cons for each in this particular situation. What are some things Sam could have done during the implementation of the program that could have resolved some of these problems?

3. Reexamine the list of the district's technology benchmarks. Be prepared to discuss how you think these benchmarks would be used by an evaluator on this project. Do you think this list is complete, or could you generate a few more? What do you see as some of the benefits for establishing these benchmarks? What do you see as some challenges or limitations of their use, particularly as they apply to this project?

CLASS ACTIVITIES

1. Taking into consideration the district's benchmarks and the logic model, develop a survey that Sam could use to administer to all teachers across the district who have participated in the last three years of technology professional development workshops.

2. What does technology integration into the classroom mean to you? Conduct some informal interviews with some teachers you know. Ask them about technology integration. What does it mean to them? Have they ever integrated technology into their classrooms?

What, if anything, have they seen from their students and or their own teaching from this experience? Were there any challenges? If so, how did they go about trying to address them? Consider how these findings would be incorporated in your evaluation report.

SUGGESTED READING

Page, M. S. (2002, Summer). Technology-enriched classrooms: Effects on students of low socioeconomic status. *Journal of Research on Technology in Education, 34*(4), 389–409.

Hopson, M. H., Simms, R. L., & Knezek, G. A. (2001–2002). Using a technology-enriched environment to improve higher-order thinking skills. *Journal of Research on Technology in Education, 34*(2), 109–119.

CHAPTER

6

EXPANSION OF A HIGH SCHOOL SCIENCE PROGRAM

LEARNING OBJECTIVES

After reading this case study you should be able to

1. Identify and understand the differences between the roles of program developers and program evaluators

2. Describe the differences between a statewide evaluation of a program and an evaluation of a program in a single facility

3. Note several barriers or challenges when expanding programs to new settings

4. Understand the important role formative evaluation feedback can play in addressing critical issues uncovered through evaluation data collection efforts

THE EVALUATORS

Jennifer Wright and Ed Abbey were internal evaluators working for an organization that sponsors science-based programs for public schools.

Although both Jennifer and Ed were based out of Washington, D.C., their evaluation work took them to locations all across the country to observe programs and collect data. One of their chief responsibilities as evaluators for the organization was to monitor various projects that the organization has funded. In some cases, Jennifer and Ed found themselves conducting *meta-evaluations*. This type of approach required that the evaluators conduct an evaluation of a single program not just in a particular school location, but across multiple locations.

THE PROGRAM

Over the past five years the organization had worked to fund an inquiry-based science program for high school students. Students participate in the program during their sophomore, junior, and senior years. The purpose of the program is to have students conduct authentic scientific research on a topic that interests them. One aspect of this approach is that the high school science teacher teaching the course serves as a facilitator to the student, making sure the student meets the required goals for the project. The teacher also meets weekly with each student and, using a portfolio that serves as an "organizer" for the student who is conducting research, confers with the student to review that week's goals and to select new goals for the student for the following week. Because students select such a wide variety of research topics, from puffins to DNA, their teachers often do not have the expertise to assist them appropriately. To address this issue, students each work with a mentor who is an expert in the chosen field of study.

THE EVALUATION PLAN

In the first three years of the project, the organization funded close to 150 school districts in one state to implement the program. As part of their internal program evaluation responsibilities, Jennifer and Ed had conducted a large-scale evaluation annually as the program expanded across the state. Box 6.1 presents an overview of the annual program evaluation plan. To execute this, Jennifer and Ed had teacher, student, administrator, and parent surveys mailed to all 150 program sites at the end of each year. These surveys collected a wide range of evaluation data for the program. In addition, Jennifer and Ed selected approximately ten programs for site visits. The evaluators spent several days on-site, conducting interviews with stakeholders (students, parents, teachers, administrators, and so on). The evaluators also reviewed materials, such as the students' portfolios, and in some cases observed students presenting their research at the school research fairs, which are open to the community.

BOX 6.1. Overview of Evaluation Objectives

1. Mail survey packet to each site; packet includes

   - Surveys for the teachers implementing the program, the school administrator, the students participating in the program, and their parents

   - Contact information collected from student mentors participating in the program and a mentor survey sent annually to the mentors

2. Make site visits to the ten schools selected annually for this and conduct the following activities:

   - Interviews with teachers implementing the program, school administrators, and parents; focus group with students

   - Review of materials and projects, including but not limited to student presentations of their research projects and their portfolios

3. Conduct site visit of annual summer training institute, have teachers complete a post-training survey, and conduct focus group interviews with teachers participating in the training.

Another effective feature of the program is its three-week summer institute for teacher training, held each year. At the institute new teachers who want to implement the program are trained by the program developers. Each week of the training is designed to simulate a year of the program. New teachers get to experience firsthand the goals and activities expected of students in the program. Over the course of the past three years the training has been very successful, with 100 percent of new teachers who were trained that summer implementing the program back at their schools in the fall.

Based on both the success of the program itself and its training, Science Away! decided to fund the project for an additional two years (years four and five). However, instead of continuing to fund program training and implementation in the one state, the organization wanted the project developers to expand the program to four different states in the next two years. Seeing this as an exciting endeavor, the project developers began to work with superintendents and state education departments in several nearby states so that they would have a ready audience. They selected a state to expand their efforts to and chose a central location for the training. Next they recruited twenty teachers and held their three-week summer training institute.

Jennifer and Ed were busy following their annual data collection methods for evaluation of the program across the state, but they made plans to visit the training site toward the end of the institute's third week. This would give them some time to observe part of the actual training that these new teachers were receiving, as well as to collect some additional data. They planned to conduct a couple of focus groups with the teachers during one of their breaks from the institute and to administer a training survey. The survey would gather teachers' perceptions about the overall quality of the training, their perceptions of their level of preparedness to implement the program a few months later in the fall, and any *barriers* or challenges teachers believed they might face in trying to implement the program back at their school building. All three of these methods—site visits, focus groups, and surveys—were the same ones Jennifer and Ed had used during the first three years of evaluating the program. From the programs implemented on the East Coast, the evaluation data had consistently revealed that following the training teachers who had not felt prepared to implement the program at the beginning of the school year typically did not implement it or failed to keep the program going once it started.

During a break in the training, the evaluators administered the survey to the teachers. Later, just before lunch, Jennifer quickly scanned the surveys. Much to her surprise, she discovered that all the teachers had indicated that they would *not* be implementing the program that coming fall.

"Ed, can I see you for a minute?" she whispered. Taking the surveys, she drew him out of the classroom and into the hallway where it was quiet.

"What's going on?"

"Take a look at the teachers' surveys," she said, handing them to him one at a time. "For the 'Yes/No' question we have about implementing for the fall academic year, everyone has checked *No*."

No wonder they were surprised: in the past *all* teachers had indicated that they *would* be implementing the program following the training.

Ed flipped through the surveys one more time just to be sure. It was true: no one was planning on implementing in the fall.

The evaluators had planned to also split the group up and conduct two group interview sessions—*focus groups*. To gather more information about this issue of delayed implementation, Jennifer and Ed decided to add a question to their focus group protocol. Later, during the two focus groups, all the teachers validated the survey finding and reaffirmed that they were not going to be implementing the program that school year. Confused, the evaluators asked the teachers why. They learned that under their state education department rules, all new curriculum adopted by school districts had to be submitted to a year-long review by the district before being adopted. This was not the case on the East Coast, where school districts could adopt any curriculum desired by the administration. The evaluators then asked the teachers if they had conveyed any of this information to the developers during the last three weeks. The teachers said that they had not told the developers because they thought they were nice people and they didn't want to upset them.

Jennifer and Ed were now faced with a dilemma. They could tell the project developers that the teachers were not going to be implementing the program in the fall as they had anticipated. However, Jennifer was worried that this information might upset the project developers, and she feared they might take it out on the teachers during the last day of training. On the other hand, if they did not tell the developers, they would go ahead and deliver the remainder of the training under the false assumption that the teachers would be implementing in the fall.

After they finished their focus groups and the teachers began to return to the training room Jennifer and Ed still did not know what they should do to resolve the situation.

SUMMARY OF EVALUATION ACTIVITIES AND FINDINGS

As with this case study, sometimes evaluators "uncover" information about the program they are studying that is critical to the overall success of the program. In this case study, Jennifer and Ed were faced with a situation wherein high school teachers being trained to implement a science program were unable to do so because of a technicality with this particular state's department of education. This had not been an issue in other states where Jennifer and Ed had evaluated the program. However, delivering that information back to project directors posed a serious challenge. Jennifer and Ed feared that the project directors might become upset at the news, which could have serious consequences for the relationship that the project developers had created with these teachers. However, by not informing the directors they would do them a disservice, in that they would continue with the remainder of the training as though the teachers were indeed planning to implement their science classes in the upcoming school year.

FINAL THOUGHTS

Program evaluation is unpredictable: evaluators never know what they are going to discover. Therefore, a successful evaluator should never take a program for granted, in that she becomes so familiar with a particular program and how it works that she uses tunnel vision in her approach. An evaluator must always be aware of the tiniest change in programming that could impact the viability of the entire program.

KEY CONCEPTS

Meta-evaluation

Barrier

 ## DISCUSSION QUESTIONS

1. What are some possible challenges that you might encounter when serving as an evaluator of a program that has been implemented at different locations around the state, as opposed to evaluating a program in a single school or district?

2. After reviewing Jennifer and Ed's evaluation plan, what are some additional evaluation activities that you think could be conducted as part of this evaluation's efforts?

3. Discovering that the teachers were not going to implement the science program in the fall was a surprise to the evaluators, forcing them to decide whether to tell the program directors during the training session. Based on what you have learned in this case study, what would you do if you were the evaluator?

CLASS ACTIVITIES

1. Often outcomes or benefits for those participating in a program go beyond the immediate scope of the program's evaluation. In this case of the high school science program, students go on to further education and careers. How, if at all, did the program assist students in their future endeavors? After reviewing the science program, generate a list of possible outcomes or benefits you think such a science program would produce for students and develop an evaluation plan for tracking these high-school students beyond the scope of the program.

2. Jennifer and Ed use a variety of tools to collect both quantitative and quantitative data. Review the evaluation plan in Box 6.1 and develop some draft instruments as though you were going to evaluate this program.

SUGGESTED READING

Duschl, R. A. (1997). Strategies and challenges to changing focus of assessment and instruction in science classrooms. *Educational Assessment, 4*(1), 37–73.

Korchin, F. G. (1997). Consumer science for the non-science high school student. *CSTA Journal,* 29–39.

CHAPTER

7

EVALUATION OF A PROVEN PRACTICE FOR READING ACHIEVEMENT

LEARNING OBJECTIVES

After reading this case study you should

1. Have a better understanding of what constitutes a proven practice versus a practice that is developed in a more naturalistic setting

2. Be able to more fully describe the processes associated with developing proven practices

3. Understand what extraneous variables are and how they can interfere with our understanding of what works and what doesn't work in the way of curriculum and instructional practices

4. Understand some of the challenges evaluators face when delivering findings and data back to clients and how this can have ramifications for all those involved in the program

THE EVALUATORS

Dennis Fuller and Margaret Lamb were both faculty members in educational psychology at a smaller teachers' college. As part of their professional work the two faculty members often worked on projects outside of the college. Dennis had an extensive background in program evaluation. He taught several courses at the college in program evaluation, and most recently his department had some extensive discussions about developing a master's program in program evaluation. Margaret had a background in educational research and literacy.

THE PROGRAM

The Reading Right program was a federally funded program geared to improve student literacy in low-performing school districts. School districts whose students had performed poorly on the state's ELA assessment were eligible to apply for these monies. Under this initiative, the Reading Right program had been noted to be a *proven practice*. A practice or activity is often referred to as "proven" when it has been subjected to a series of studies involving experimental or quasi-experimental design. To control for *extraneous variables*—that is, variables that may be making a more significant impact than the actual program itself—these studies are conducted in very controlled, sometimes laboratory-like settings. In repeated lab trials, with students who had low literacy competencies, the Reading Right curriculum had made noticeable and significant improvements.

The *funding cycle* or timeline for the federal funding was two years. However, districts could submit for another round of possible funding to extend the initiative to a total of four years. As part of that extension process, an external evaluation of the program was required. This evaluation was multifold; Box 7.1 presents some evaluation questions that had to be answered.

It was also a requirement under the grant that all eligible schools implement the Reading Right program—failure to do so would result in the district's no longer receiving funding. For the evaluation, Dennis and Margaret were hired by an urban district that had received two years of Reading Right funding and was reapplying for an extension of additional years. In this district there were seven elementary schools; all were eligible and had been implementing Reading Right. The district superintendent, who had hired Dennis and Margaret, was adamant in ensuring that all the elementary schools were implementing Reading Right. He told the evaluators that if a school was not implementing the program

---

BOX 7.1. **Evaluation Questions for the Reading Right Program**

1. How is the program being implemented across the schools?

2. Is it being correctly implemented at all sites?

3. What are administrator, teacher, and staff perceptions of the program?

4. Do these stakeholders see any benefits to students as a result of implementing the Reading Right program?

5. Do they see any challenges with its implementation?

6. Has student performance in literacy on the state's ELA assessment improved?

---

correctly, he wanted to know and have the school named in the evaluation report so they could work with the school to improve the program's implementation.

THE EVALUATION PLAN

To answer the evaluation questions, Dennis and Margaret began to collect both quantitative and qualitative data. They created a survey that went out to all teachers, administrators, and staff at the seven elementary buildings. They also collected school data on student performance on the ELA. In addition to collecting data for test years that corresponded to program implementation, they decided to also collect *baseline data* or preliminary data for three years prior to the implementation of Reading Right. Finally, they developed interview protocols and began to meet with teachers one-to-one and in small groups. The purpose of the interviews was to gather more in-depth data from teachers about the Reading Right curriculum and how they went about implementing it.

SUMMARY OF EVALUATION ACTIVITIES AND FINDINGS

In six of the elementary schools Dennis and Margaret found that the Reading Right curriculum was being implemented with fidelity, meaning that its procedures, activities, and assessments were being followed according to the curriculum guidelines and procedure manuals. Dennis and Margaret found that these schools had made no notable gains in student performance following their implementation of Reading Right when compared to the baseline data. One district out of the seven had made some impressive gains with increasing student performance on the ELA assessment over the course of the past two years. However, during the interviews with teachers from this district it was revealed that the teachers were not using the Reading Right curriculum. Teachers told the evaluation team that they "pretended" to use the Reading Right curriculum, and they had all the materials available in their classrooms. However, the teachers reported, when they closed their doors they "did their own thing." The teachers noted that over the past few years they had developed their own curriculum, based on what they found to work with their students in their classes. During the interviews teachers referred to it as a "grassroots" reading curriculum. And they were not about to give it up and use a curriculum, like Reading Right, that they didn't know much about and didn't really know would even work for their students.

Afterward, Margaret and Dennis discussed their findings. What were they to do? If they reported the findings that the one elementary school wasn't implementing the program, the whole district would be in jeopardy of losing the funding. In addition, the superintendent would know which school wasn't implementing the proven practice and would want to change what the teachers were doing. Ironically, it was this school that had made the only gains in ELA over the past couple of years.

What were Margaret and Dennis to do?

After much debate, in the end, Margaret and Dennis reported that the Reading Right curriculum was not being implemented with fidelity to the model in the one elementary school. However, they pointed out, this was the only school that had made notable gains in student performance on the ELA. They also made recommendations for the district to further study the curriculum that teachers were delivering to students in that elementary school. Because grades across the other six schools did not vary much from the initial baseline, school board members were leery of continuing with the Reading Right curriculum, despite the large amount of grant funds they would be able to obtain from the federal government. Instead, the district had the evaluation team conduct further investigation into the one elementary school and break down the grassroots curriculum that these teachers had created from years of experience on the job. Shortly afterward, the state education department posted an RFP to improve low performance in the ELA. The district submitted a grant proposal based on the grassroots curriculum in the one elementary school. It received a large grant to continue to train teachers in other schools using this curriculum. As the district moved the curriculum into the other schools, slowly student ELA performance increased there as well.

FINAL THOUGHTS

At first glance, the idea of a "proven practice" is admittedly attractive. However, as our evaluators discovered, sometimes it is not the proven practice that is making the change or impact occur, but a combination of this practice and other extraneous variables working together. Often a practice or particular method will be credited with improving an educational setting when that credit should actually go to the dedicated administrators, teachers, and staff members whose hard work of "wrapping around" the practice or program have put it in place. When other districts see such improvement they too want to adopt such practices, only to find that these practices produce less than satisfactory results when they are implemented as originally intended.

KEY CONCEPTS

Proven practice

Extraneous variables

Funding cycle

Baseline data

DISCUSSION QUESTIONS

1. Pretend for a moment that you are Margaret or Dennis. What would you do if you were the evaluator on the project? How might you go about delivering the information from your evaluation to the district superintendent and the school board? What other concerns would you have with delivering this information?

2. Evaluators often collect different kinds of information and data. For example, Margaret and Dennis collected both qualitative and quantitative data. They examined the districts' actual ELA test data during the time the Reading Right program was occurring, as well as three years prior to the program's implementation. They referred

to this as *baseline data*. Why is collecting this baseline data important? Without it, what might be some ramifications that could interfere with the evaluation findings?

3. In the discussion about proven practice and establishing a proven practice in a lablike setting, the term *extraneous variables* is brought up. What are some extraneous variables that might show change in literacy but share no relationship or connection with the Reading Right program?

CLASS ACTIVITIES

1. Margaret and Dennis developed several instruments in conducting their evaluations. Based on what you have learned in the case study, develop a draft of a survey and interview protocol they might have used in gathering data about the Reading Right program from across the seven elementary schools.

2. One of the goals of the evaluation is to determine whether the Reading Right program is being delivered appropriately, according to how it was created and delivered in the lab-like studies. How, as an evaluator, do you think you might go about doing this?

3. At the end of the case study it is revealed that the district has decided to go ahead and expand the curriculum that was shown to be successful in the one elementary school. Based on that narrative, if you were evaluating the expansion of this program, how might you go about conducting such an evaluation? Develop an initial plan and evaluation matrix that you or your group can present to the class.

SUGGESTED READING

Beswick, J. F., Willams, D. J., & Sloat, E. A. (2005). A comparative study of teacher ratings of emergent literacy skills and student performance on a standardized measure. *Education*, *126*(1), 317–382.

Simmons, D. C., et al. (2007). *Journal of Learning Disabilities*, *40*(4), 331–347.

CHAPTER

8

PROJECT PLAN FOR EVALUATION OF A STATEWIDE AFTER-SCHOOL INITIATIVE

LEARNING OBJECTIVES

After reading this case study you should be able to

1. Demonstrate the various benefits and challenges of conducting a large statewide evaluation

2. Understand different approaches or models for delivering after-school, enrichment-oriented programming

3. Explain what is meant by the term *higher collaboration of services*

4. Explain what is meant by the term *partner* in relation to collaboration among different agencies

5. Develop a plan for conducting a statewide evaluation of an after-school program that addresses some of the technical and methodological issues inherent in this type of evaluation practice

99

THE EVALUATORS

Tina Larson and her colleagues formed a small consultancy. In recent years, with the increase in school accountability, the amount of evaluation work had increased exponentially. Although the firm worked on a wide variety of projects, a substantial portion of its revenue came from competitive grants. These projects usually took the form of RFPs, whereby the evaluator worked collaboratively with a school district, agency, or group to evaluate a single project for them. In cases of RFPs, many school districts might receive awards to implement their proposed projects. Although bids often followed the same process, they usually resulted in only one award being given. Often state agencies or groups put a bid out looking to hire an evaluator or evaluation firm for a specific project.

The firm now needed to respond to a state RFP. The state would be reviewing proposals for a *statewide evaluation* of all the after-school programs the state had funded under this effort and would issue one contract for the group that provided the best overall comprehensive evaluation plan. The deadline for the bid was in a week. Although Tina had informally discussed aspects of the proposed evaluation plan with members of her firm, the group had set aside a couple of hours to meet and flesh out their ideas for their proposal.

THE PROGRAM

For the previous eight years, after-school programming had been a main focus for the state's education department. During this time the state provided funding to approximately 150 school districts across the state. As part of the programmatic structure, after-school programs funded under these efforts had a certain *model* or structure for serving students. Prior to this funding initiative many school districts had historically provided their own after-school programming to their students. However, because these programs were expensive to operate, only affluent districts were able to offer such services to their student body. The advent of the state's *competitive funds*—grants for which eligible school districts competed through the RFP process—made it possible for many high-need school districts to deliver a rich array of programming.

Although this initiative had many goals, one major goal of after-school programming is generally to decrease incidents of violence and crime-related behaviors associated with students and school dismissals.

Another program goal was to decrease student misbehaviors during the school day and to increase student academic performance in classroom learning and on the state's standardized annual assessments.

Another main component of after-school programming is the *curriculum* or set of activities being provided, with high-quality programs offering an array of activities. Box 8.1 presents a listing of some of those broad categories.

BOX 8.1. Overview of Broad Categories for After-School Programming

Arts and crafts	Book Club
Music	Chess Club
Dance	Science Club
Cooking (home and careers)	Journalism Club

In addition, after-school programs are required to provide assistance to help students improve their academic performance. Parent and community involvement are also a main component of high-quality after-school programs under this model. In addition, these programs are supposed to provide academic enrichment for parents through parenting classes and degree work (such as the General Educational Diploma or GED).

One distinctive aspect of this particular program was the way in which the activities were provided. The program required school districts to *partner* or collaborate with those services or agencies in their communities (such as YMCA or Boys and Girls Club). These agencies or groups generally have a long-standing history in their communities for providing high-quality after-school programming. Other partners that could be involved include 4-H programs, local libraries, nature centers, and museums. Figure 8.1 gives an overview of one after-school program's structure.

As mentioned earlier, traditionally some schools have offered after-school programming. However, for many schools that do not have the resources or the expertise to provide such programming, students have

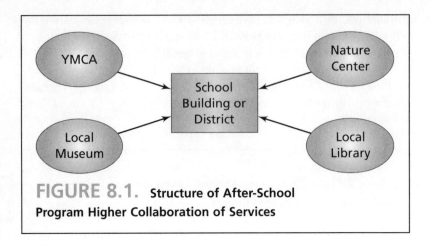

FIGURE 8.1. **Structure of After-School Program Higher Collaboration of Services**

traditionally either left their school premises at the end of the day to attend such programs elsewhere or returned to a home unsupervised by an adult.

As depicted in Figure 8.1, the students involved no longer go to after-school programming; instead the programming, for the most part, comes to them at their school building. This particular model is often referred to in the field of program development and evaluation as a *higher collaboration of services*, meaning that instead of an individual having to go to several services, the services themselves are provided together as one or in such a way that it is easier for individuals to receive the services. In addition to these types of activities and partners, a school could also incorporate summer programming to provide quality year-round services to students and the community.

THE INITIAL CHALLENGE

Everyone from Tina's group came to the planning meeting having read the requirements in the RFP. Tina decided that she would facilitate the meeting. In years past, the firm had served as an evaluator for several individual school districts that had provided after-school programming under the state's initiative. As a result, Tina had built some solid understanding of these after-school programs—how they function and how they are structured at the individual school level.

The consensus among the group's members was that they were interested in the firm's bidding on the statewide proposal. In general, the firm had mainly focused on conducting individual school evaluations, whereby they were working directly for a school district or agency and evaluated a single program. However, everyone in the firm realized that a statewide project such as this would surely bring a great deal of recognition to the growing firm and would no doubt lead to other large-scale evaluation projects down the road.

The group decided that they would discuss some of the bigger methodological issues of the project first. Overall, the purpose of the statewide evaluation was to determine whether this after-school programming initiative had any effect on students' performance in school and decreased incidents of violent behavior in the immediate school community. This aspect of the project was very clear to the members of the firm. But *how* an evaluation plan would go about trying to show if such change occurred still remained somewhat of a challenge.

"What we really want to do in the evaluation plan is to show, wherever possible, that the after-school programming worked," said Ben, the executive director of the firm.

"I agree, and we can start to do this by examining the relationship between number of student attendances in their respective after-school programs and correlate it to student performance and incidents of violent behavior for each student involved," said Stan, a member of the firm's measurement and statistics department.

Tina had let the others talk first. Now she chimed in: "Well, ultimately, yes, that's what we want to do as evaluators, but the big question is how?"

Joan, another member of the stats department, springboarded from Stan's idea: "We could assess each program's student attendance records. According to the state, it is mandatory that funded programs keep careful records of student attendance. Like Stan suggested, we could start there, and correlate the attendance data with other variables such as the state's standardized test in English language arts or math."

"That makes total sense," said Kara, a new employee fresh out of a master's program in educational research and statistics. "Think of the after-school program as the independent variable [IV] or treatment—correlating these two variables would help to show that the more of the IV students received, the higher their scores were on certain tests."

"That would make sense and help to show that the after-school programs were doing something," said Joan.

"I like it," said Ben, half-listening to the conversation as he text messaged a prospective client on his cell phone about the next day's meeting.

"How about if we even found some students in each school or district that were to participate in the after-school program but chose not to, so they didn't receive any? They could serve as a sort of comparison group."

"That would show even more evidence that the programs were making an impact," said Stan. He scribbled a few notes on a legal pad.

The group continued with the discussion, talking about different correlations that they could run and possible comparisons of data sets to help show cause-effect relationships. Finally Tina interrupted, "These are all interesting ideas, but I think we are overlooking a major problem."

The room fell silent; all eyes turned toward her.

"How so?" asked Stan.

Tina felt a slight tightness in her throat. But she was confident in relying on her past experience in evaluating these programs to help support her point. "Well, the plan that you are talking about to evaluate the programs assumes that all the programs function the same way."

"What?" Stan stopped taking notes. Ben also stopped his text messaging and put down his cell phone.

Tina went on, "You are assuming that all the hundred and fifty or so after-school programs the state has funded all function the same way. But that is just not the case. The firm has evaluated several school districts that received funding from the state and even though it is part of the same initiative and the programs are all required to have the same overall goals and objectives, they went about structuring their programs and delivering activities very differently."

Tina went on to explain that one variable where programs may differ was in the partners they employed. In some cases, she noted, school districts used a combination of partners (as depicted in Figure 8.1). However, depending on the community agencies and after-school programming groups in a certain area, those partnerships that make up the program could look very different. In addition, even though the school districts kept careful records regarding student attendance, the type of activities that schools could offer as part of their programming—as well as the type of activities that students chose to do—could and did vary. For example, one school's after-school program may have focused heavily on the performing arts, while a neighboring school's program may have had a science or engineering focus. In addition, another school may not have a theme or focus, and students may select from a "menu" of after-school programming activities. Tina also explained that even though most of the state's after-school programming initiative focused on elementary and middle schools, some districts' program were also implemented in high school. And she noted that even if schools did implement that exact same program, the funding awards that each school received could be and were different.

"How could you compare an elementary school that received $100,000 for programming and the same program in another elementary building that received $500,000?" she asked. "I just think there are too many variables, too many assumptions that have to be made in order to look at this thing in our usual way."

No one said a word, except Ben. He picked up his cell phone and called his secretary, telling her to cancel the rest of his appointments for the day.

"In reality, folks," Tina continued, "we could be looking at a hundred and fifty different ways to offer after-school programming."

Faced with this new information, the members of the firm had a new concern. Now they were worried not about *how* to conduct a statewide evaluation across multiple after-school programs, but whether they even *could*.

THE EVALUATION PLAN

Tina and her colleagues were determined to produce a competitive proposal for the contract bid for the state's evaluation of the after-school programming initiative. Based on the new information that Tina brought to the table, the group began to work out a possible strategy for collecting data. The group decided that they first needed to identify after-school programs that had similar characteristics (for example, same grade levels, same hours of operation, similar partners from the community, similar curriculum). They decided to obtain this information by proposing to first design and develop a survey. The survey would be filled out by the director of the after-school programs. They would mail a survey to each of the 150 or so funded sites around the state. Then they would analyze this data and, based on their findings, identify those districts that implemented after-school programming in the same way. Next they would begin to examine correlations between students in those similar programs and academic achievement and the other outcomes associated with the program. Finally, they planned to examine the achievement of similar, comparable students who were eligible for attending after-school programming but did not.

FINAL THOUGHTS

Several months later Tina received a phone call from the state's evaluation and assessment office congratulating the firm on their successful application. Shortly thereafter, the firm met with several directors from the state who were charged with the statewide after-school project, and the team began to put their evaluation plan into place.

KEY CONCEPTS

Statewide evaluation

Model

Competitive funds

Curriculum

Partner

Higher collaboration of services

DISCUSSION QUESTIONS

1. One challenge the evaluation team faced when placing their bid was the different ways in which the after-school programs could be implemented across the different sites. Review the case study again; what do you see as some of the benefits and challenges to how after-school activities were conducted traditionally in many communities? What are some of the benefits and challenges to how after-school programs are conducted under the new model depicted in Figure 8.1?

2. The term *higher collaboration of services* is mentioned in this case study. In relation to how after-school programming can be provided, this refers to the process whereby "partners" come to the school or setting and deliver their services. Review the case again and be prepared to discuss why the term has been applied to program structures such as the one found in Figure 8.1. What makes it a higher collaboration of services? With what areas could you see this type of program model working well? Please be ready to explain.

CLASS ACTIVITIES

Based on the case study and the methods discussed to evaluate the program under its conditions, develop some of the evaluation tools that will be needed. For example, develop the survey that will be administered to all the funded sites or develop an interview protocol that could be used for the site visits that will be conducted under the evaluation plan.

SUGGESTED READING

Mahoney, J. L., Pavente, M. E., & Lord, H. (2007). After-school program engagement: Links to child competency and program quality and content. *Elementary School Journal, 107*(4), 385–404.

McGarrell, E. F. (2007). Characteristics of effective and ineffective after-school programs. *Criminology & Public Policy, 6*(2), 283–288.

Zhang, J. J., Lam, E. T. C., Smith, D. W., Fleming, D. S., & Connaughton, D. P. (2006). Development of the scale for program facilitators to assess the effectiveness of after-school achievement programs. *Measurement in Physical Education and Exercise Science, 10*(3), 151–167.

CHAPTER

9

EVALUATION OF A TRAINING PROGRAM IN MATHEMATICS FOR TEACHERS

LEARNING OBJECTIVES

After reading this case study you should be able to

1. Understand what professional development is and several approaches to its implementation

2. Understand why a needs assessment is conducted and each step of its process

3. Define what action research is and the steps associated with it

4. Define what a semistructured interview is and the kind of important data that can be collected

THE EVALUATORS

Barbara Lincoln and Seth Jackson were professional evaluators. They generally worked independently, conducting evaluations and other consulting activities. However, on certain occasions when a program evaluation project warranted, they would team up and work collaboratively.

Barbara was a former professor in educational theory and practice and had an extensive background in action research and qualitative methods. Seth, too, had retired from a long and successful career in education as a math educator. Both Barbara and Seth were hired to serve as evaluators on professional development project for middle school teachers in math instruction.

THE PROGRAM

The program was designed to assist poorly performing school districts in the area of mathematics by providing quality, ongoing professional development. As part of this process, institutions of higher education (IHEs) would link to and collaborate with identified districts and use expert faculty in the area of mathematics and learning to provide such professional development training. In all, four IHEs and thirteen school districts made up the program. Under this program design, teachers from each participating district participated in weekend professional development trainings provided at each IHE. These trainings were held on Saturdays every other month, across the academic year, and teachers were paid a stipend for their participation in the project. To provide professional development aligned to the needs of the individual teachers, the project director and IHE faculty worked to conduct a *needs assessment*—a systematic data collection process that identifies an issue or issues that need to be addressed by the organization or group, rather than making an arbitrary decision. The needs assessment entailed reviewing each participating district's math assessment data for the last four years at the fifth-grade level and conducting an *item analysis* of items students had answered incorrectly, to see if there were any notable patterns among or across schools, classrooms, teachers. Based on the item analysis, a series of professional development trainings were then developed specifically to target the identified deficiencies.

In years one through three of the project, approximately one hundred teachers had received professional development training in these areas of need. In addition, the teachers had received numerous supplies and materials (such as algebra tiles, a hands-on manipulative) to bring back to their classroom and implement to assist students in their learning. As part of the year four activities, Barbara and Seth began to conduct their evaluation activities by attending the professional development training. One of their main data collection models during the trainings was observations. Both Barbara and Seth wanted to get a real feel for the kinds of activities that were being conducted, to better understand the approach and rapport the professional development trainers had with the teachers and to be better able to fully describe what these trainings were like.

THE EVALUATION PLAN

These are some of Barbara and Seth's initial questions:

1. Were these trainings targeting the right strategies?

2. Did teachers find the sessions informative and useful?

3. Did teachers believe that they would be able to implement the strategies they were being trained in when they returned to their classrooms?

In addition, Barbara and Seth wanted to conduct some semistructured interviews with training participants. Unlike structured interviews, in which one closely follows a protocol, a semistructured format allowed the evaluators the flexibility to conduct short, informal interviews whenever there was a break in the training (such as during coffee breaks). Using a more formal approach, Barbara and Seth also planned to collect end-of-year data from participating teachers through focus groups and a survey. This summative survey would work to document the following data:

■ The various professional development activities teachers participated in

■ Any changes in their instruction through implementing these new practices

■ Any challenges these teachers may have encountered

■ Any benefits or outcomes teachers observed in their students when they implemented these strategies

In addition, Barbara and Seth planned to visit teachers' classrooms and to observe students as they were introduced to the new math strategies.

IMPLEMENTING THE EVALUATION PLAN

During one of their breakout seminars, Barbara made an interesting discovery while chatting informally with a group of teachers standing in line for coffee.

"The strategy using the algebra tiles to show how to multiply positive and negative numbers sounds very useful, doesn't it?" She asked them.

"I guess," said one of the teachers.

"I don't think my kids would be able to get this at all," said another teacher.

"I know mine wouldn't," chimed in a third.

Barbara took a sip of her coffee and looked around to see where Seth was. She wanted him to hear this. "Well, what about the other strategies that you have learned about? How have they worked?"

No one responded.

Then one of the teachers shrugged her shoulders and said, "I don't know, I've never really been able to try things. It always seems that they never really fit into what I'm teaching."

"I know what you mean," interjected the second teacher. "It's really hard to stop what I have planned to cover in class and try out this month's strategy from the training."

Barbara was surprised at what she was hearing. Careful not to show any concern, she said, "So it sounds as though you haven't had great success trying these different strategies."

In a chorus all the teachers replied, "No."

Barbara could barely wait until lunch to inform Seth about her discovery. When she told him, he confessed that he had made a similar finding: very few of the teachers were going back to their schools and implementing any of the strategies with their students.

At the end of the day the project director held a meeting with Barbara and Seth and the faculty members who had been conducting the training. The purpose of the meeting was to discuss evaluation findings, how they thought the training was going, and what activities they wanted to focus on in the next year of the project. During the meeting, when it came time for Barbara and Seth to speak, Barbara delivered the news, based on the semistructured interviews they had conducted.

"Impossible," said the project director. He picked up a stack of surveys that the teachers had filled out at the end of the day and began to thumb through them. "Teachers have indicated in their surveys that they have been going back and using these strategies in their classrooms."

Everyone turned to Barbara and Seth.

Seth broke the silence by saying, "Participants don't always provide valid data on surveys."

"I don't know," said the project director. "I think that the teachers have always been pretty honest with us."

"I'm not too sure about that," said one of the faculty members, who was in charge of delivering the professional development. "I have to agree with the evaluators. From what I have been experiencing during the workshops, it appears that the teachers really aren't embracing these strategies as we had once hoped."

Now the project director looked completely perplexed. "Well, so what do we do now?"

"We need to make them do it," said one of the trainers.

"We could withhold their stipends unless they can show us that they are using it," said the director.

"Or we could recruit new people into the training and phase out those teachers that aren't fully participating," said another of the trainers.

Barbara and Seth looked at each other. With their rich background in program evaluation, they knew all too well that trying to force participants to comply was an approach that would most likely spell disaster. How exactly they could get teachers involved was going to be a major challenge—but extremely important if the project was going to carry on, be successful, and meet all of its intended goals and objectives.

SUMMARY OF EVALUATION ACTIVITIES AND FINDINGS

Following the meeting, it was clear to everyone that the method with which they had been delivering professional development training to the teachers was not as effective as they had once hoped or believed it to be.

Barbara and Seth returned home for several days to discuss ideas for how they could get the teachers more involved in the project and implementing the strategies they had learned about. More important, they also discussed ways in which they could do this that would not follow a *top-down approach*. As depicted in Figure 9.1, in this approach, typically those in an administrative or higher-level position will control or dictate what needs to be done when and for what purpose. As Barbara and Seth closely examined this professional development model, they realized that it placed all the emphasis on the professional development training itself, putting it on top or at a higher level than the teachers who were receiving it. The teachers may have felt as though the professional development training was "being done to them" rather than their being given a meaningful role in the process.

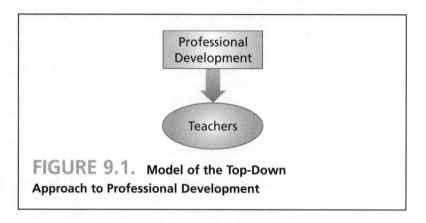

FIGURE 9.1. **Model of the Top-Down Approach to Professional Development**

The following week Barbara and Seth meet with the project director and trainers. First they presented the top-down model as the way the professional development had been structured for the last three years of the project. They pointed out some of the inherent challenges with such a model, particularly from an empowerment perspective. Then they unveiled the new model that they had developed for the following year's program (see Figure 9.2).

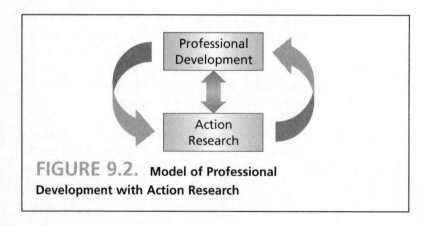

FIGURE 9.2. **Model of Professional Development with Action Research**

In their new model, Barbara had incorporated her love for *action research* (see Box 9.1). This new model incorporated the basic element of action research while continuing the element of professional development that the project was built on. Using the action research model, teachers who had participated in the project were asked to take a strategy that they had learned about over the course of the three years of professional development and conduct an action research project. The teachers would serve as the researchers, conducting authentic research in their own classrooms to improve instructional practices and maximize student learning. They would either analyze some current data or implement a pretest measure. They were to introduce the strategy over the course of a few days and then test students on whatever unit they deemed appropriate. Then they would examine the post-test assessments for students, determine whether an acceptable level of learning had occurred, and, if not, modify the strategy, implement the refined strategy once again, and continue to collect data and make modifications until the desired learning outcome was achieved.

Next, teachers would report their data, findings, reflections, and even their recommendations back to the professional development trainers, who would be sitting on a panel, listening to the presentation of action-research projects and asking questions.

BOX 9.1. Overview of Action Research

There are many approaches to action research, but the general process tends to be the same in all of them. Figure 9.3 depicts the general process, described by Lodico et al. (2006), whereby the teacher-researcher identifies a problem or issues that need to be addressed, reviews multiple sources and forms of data, and reflects on his or her own teaching practices. Following the analysis of these data, the teacher develops a plan to address the problem, implements the plan, and then continues to collect data to monitor the plan, refining it as necessary. One of the advantages of action research is that the application of findings discovered from the research is readily adopted by the teacher-researcher.

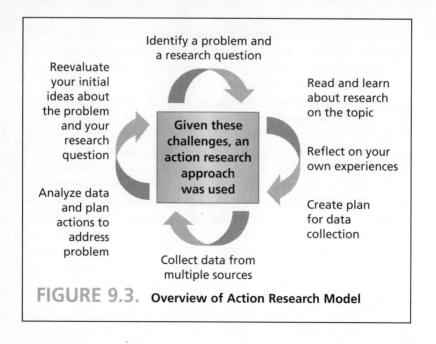

FIGURE 9.3. **Overview of Action Research Model**

After Barbara and Seth had finished presenting the model, the project director said, "I like it a lot. In a way, it does kind of force teachers to try out one of the strategies we have taught them."

"And it does it in such an interesting way," added one of the trainers. "It puts some of the responsibility for trying these strategies on them, but at the same time *empowers* them by giving them a *voice.*"

"Well," said the project director, rubbing his hands together, "let's try it and see if it works."

FINAL THOUGHTS

A couple of months later, Barbara and Seth presented the idea of incorporating the action research component to the teachers. Illustrating the concept with a PowerPoint presentation, they explained what action research was and how the project was going to incorporate it, so that it would now be the teachers' turn to provide data to the program trainers. After the presentation, the project director and trainers described how the teachers had responded as they were watching the presentation. They had begun to sit up straighter in their chairs with smiles on their faces.

The following month's training was dramatically different from the previous training. Teachers presented their action research projects and the results to their colleagues and trainers. Most of the teachers who implemented a strategy in their classrooms had found, to their surprise, that their students had great success with it. In some cases that success did not completely meet the teacher's expectations, but the teachers were already making modifications to the strategy and continuing to monitor as they implemented them. Both the project director and trainers were impressed with how much more invested the teachers were, the intricate data the teachers were collecting on their students, and the effectiveness of these professional development practices.

As part of their evaluation efforts, Barbara and Seth used the teachers' case studies in their evaluation report. In fact, the action research component embedded in a professional development model attracted the interest of the state department of education, who funded the project. They enjoyed it so much that they later hired Barbara and Seth to work with another professional development project that had encountered similar difficulties in getting teachers to implement and share new instructional practices.

KEY CONCEPTS

Needs assessment

Item analysis

Top-down approach

Action research

DISCUSSION QUESTIONS

1. Review the two different models for professional development used in this project and be prepared to discuss some of the benefits and challenges that a program evaluator might face in working with a client to deliver both approaches.

2. Be prepared to list the different steps of the needs assessment process used for this project and to explain why such a process is important.

3. What is action research, and what are the steps in conducting an action research process? How are these steps similar to or different from those of a needs assessment or research study?

4. What are some of the benefits and challenges of using semistructured interviews as a method for collecting data? And how does an

evaluator make sense of information when data from two different methods (such as survey and interview) do not complement one another?

5. Evaluators often come on board with a project that is already in operation, as did Barbara and Seth. Develop a list of different approaches or techniques that you believe would work to foster and build relationships with project directors, staff, and other relevant stakeholder groups when starting a project such as this.

CLASS ACTIVITIES

1. Review both the program goals and evaluation activities again. Based on this information, develop an evaluation matrix to ensure that all essential evaluation data is being collected, and suggest additional methodologies to address any gaps in the data collection process that you uncover.

2. The approach that Barbara and Seth took with their evaluation plan certainly worked to empower the teachers. Reflecting on this and other evaluation projects you have either worked on or learned about, develop a list of other possible techniques that an evaluator can use to foster empowerment of participants in a program.

SUGGESTED READING

Feldman, A. (2007). Teachers, responsibility, and action research. *Educational Action Research, 15*(2), 239–252.

Luckcock, T. (2007). Theoretical resource: The soul of teaching and professional learning: an appreciative inquiry into the Enneagram of reflective practice. *Educational Action Research, 15*(1), 127–145.

Thompson, P. (2007). Developing classroom talk through practitioner research. *Educational Action Research, 15*(1), 41–60.

CHAPTER

10

EVALUATORS-IN-TRAINING: ISSUES OF CONFIDENTIALITY

LEARNING OBJECTIVES

After reading this case study you should be able to

1. Define what is meant by the term *confidentiality* in program evaluation

2. Understand some of the challenges evaluators encounter when trying to maintain confidentiality for participants in the evaluation process

3. Understand some of the challenges that evaluators face in obtaining accurate data when observing participants in a program

THE EVALUATORS

Shirah Smith was a doctoral candidate in educational psychology at a state university. As part of her course work she had also taken several classes in program evaluation. For her practicum she was required to work for a faculty member at the university on an actual program evaluation project. Shirah made an appointment with the faculty member to get a better sense of the program she would be working on and what the project would entail.

THE PROGRAM

At their meeting, her professor, Dr. Dana Nephews, gave Shirah some introductory materials. "Here is an overview of the project that we are currently working on. It's an advocacy program at a middle school. Are you familiar with advocacy programs?"

As part of her doctoral experience Shirah had worked on several different kinds of programs, including after-school programming and other similar enrichment programs. However, she had never come across a program called *advocacy* before. "Is it an enrichment program?" she asked.

The professor handed her some more papers. "Yes, I guess it could be considered enrichment of some sort. One main purpose of the program is that it provides students with an adult mentor—an advocate, I guess you could say. Each student in the building is assigned to an adult. The adult probably serves as advocate for three or four students. The adult meets with the assigned students for twenty-five minutes each morning, in place of home room, and they discuss different current events and any problems that the students are having."

"How do they have enough teachers to cover all the students?" asked Shirah.

"Good question. That was one of my initial questions too when we started," said Professor Nephews. "It's not just teachers who are serving as advocates, but anyone employed at the school."

"Do you mean staff members, too?"

"Yes, even the school administrator has a handful of students that meet in his office every morning to discuss current topics."

"That's very interesting," said Shirah.

"It really is," said the professor. "The idea is that every adult will know several students very well and be able to assist if a student is having social or emotional problems."

The professor explained other aspects of the program. For example, the advocacy program also had a community-service component, whereby on weekends students would help out elderly people in the neighborhood, raking their lawns and performing other such tasks.

"It sounds like a great program," said Shirah.

"It is," said the professor, "but I also have to warn you about something."

"What?"

"Some of the teachers in the school do not like the program and don't necessarily want the program at the school."

"Really? Why?"

"We aren't sure," said Professor Nephews. "We didn't become aware of this until we became more involved in the program and started spending more time interviewing the teachers. There is this core of teachers who feel that the program is violating a contractual issue and that the program is really being forced on them by the principal. These are also teachers who are not tenured and therefore feel that if they don't fully participate and embrace the program it will come back to haunt them."

"And so the principal would deny them tenure because they don't like the advocacy program?"

The professor shrugged her shoulders. "I know it seems unlikely, but they are scared. Their perceptions are very real. We can't deny them that."

"Have you talked to the principal about this—how these teachers feel?" asked Shirah.

Professor Nephew took out a pencil and made a few notes on her legal pad. "That is one of the problems that I wanted to warn you about."

"The principal?"

"Yes, we have had some problems initially with him. Well, I shouldn't say *problems*; they were more like concerns, really."

"Concerns?"

"Yes." Professor Nephews finished taking her notes and looked back up at Shirah. "When we initially made this discovery in the evaluation—that some of the nontenured teachers did not like the program but felt that they couldn't be forthright with how they felt because they feared some sort of retaliation—we reported the findings in our first evaluation report. We protected the teachers' confidentiality by *aggregating* or combining our findings, saying 'some teachers' interviewed said this."

"So what is the problem?"

"Well, the problem is now the principal is on a sort of 'witch hunt' trying to find out who among the teachers feels this way."

"Wow," said Shirah. "It sounds intense. Are you sure you want me to get involved in this?"

"Yes, of course. I didn't mean to put you off the project by telling you all of this. I just thought you should know so that you will be extra careful in regard to maintaining participants' confidentiality. It's a wonderful program, and I think it will be a good learning experience for you."

THE EVALUATION PLAN

The evaluation plan for the project included the use of both quantitative and qualitative methods. As part of their evaluation duties, the evaluation team surveyed all teachers and staff in the building and conducted interviews and focus groups with both the students and the advocates. They also conducted some informal observations of the students and their advocates during the first twenty-five minutes of school, a period dedicated to the advocacy program. The evaluators also designed and developed a survey to gather the perceptions of those teachers, administrators, staff, and volunteers who were serving as advocates in the program.

Shirah worked with Professor Nephews to set up several observations of advocates and their meetings with students each morning. One of the purposes of conducting these observations was to give Shirah and the other evaluators the opportunity to learn more about the project and what specific activities were conducted during these advocacy sessions. This information would not only serve as rich data for the overall evaluation report but would enable the evaluators to write rich, detailed narratives describing these activities in depth for the evaluation report.

To conduct the observations, Shirah sat in on several sessions taking notes and listening to the group discussions. In one session the students were talking to their advocate about a community project that they had participated in the weekend before. They were telling their advocate about the activity, in which they had visited the homes of the elderly in the community and did odd jobs for them. From the conversations they were having, Shirah began an informal list of the specific jobs the students mentioned. Box 10.1 presents the list she started to compose.

From talking about these activities, students also had a discussion about how providing this help to the elderly made them feel about themselves. Students also talked about a safety issue in school that was on the front page of that day's newspaper. The article discussed school safety policies and an incident in which a fifth grader brought a gun to school. Shirah noted that the students talked at length about the article, how they had concerns about their own safety at the school and on the bus, and how they knew several students who in the past had brought knives to school.

BOX 10.1. Sampling of Community Activities

Rake lawns

Clean outside windows

Mulch flower beds

Trim hedges

Plant flowers

Mend a broken fence

Collect dead tree limbs off the lawn

Collect rocks for a rock garden

Fix broken door

Remove winter windows and put in summer window screens

After each observation Shirah summarized her notes, and at the end of the week she met with her professor to *debrief* or review her findings. As part of this process Professor Nephews also had Shirah reflect on what she had discovered and learned from the process, as well as generate new questions from the observations that she now wanted to have answered.

"These morning advocacy sessions that I have been observing seem very powerful," said Shirah, flipping through her notes.

"How so?" replied her professor.

"The rich conversations that I have observed between the advocates and the students—they have been discussing some serious issues and reflecting on them in their own school. Students have also been able to relate and discuss those issues in their own lives and at school." Shirah went on to describe the discussion about school safety and several students' knowing of others who had brought knives into school.

"So it sounds as though from what you have observed it's all quite positive."

"Definitely," replied Shirah. "And what's puzzling is why some teachers would find the program troublesome and not part of their job."

"I think it's a very complex issue," said Professor Nephews. "But just in what you described to me about the school safety issue, I think the teachers who are 'anti' the program are uncomfortable because they aren't quite sure what their role is."

"What do you mean?"

"I think because the program is occurring during school hours, during their traditional homeroom time, teacher-advocates feel that students are going to divulge information to them in these rich conversations that they in turn will have to report."

"Hmmm, I didn't think about it that way." Shirah sat back in her chair and made a few notes on her pad.

"The example of the issues surrounding school safety is a perfect one," said Professor Nephews. "Students said that they knew of other students who had brought knives to school. What if students were to mention specific names of students? Or talk about other things regarding their personal safety, such as abuse? That moves it from a discussion between students and the advocate to something the advocate will have to report to a higher authority such as the building principal."

Shirah thought for a moment, then said, "So those teachers who are against the program may feel it's putting them in a very difficult position?"

"I think so," said Professor Nephews. "And I think it is particularly concerning them because the program itself places them in a potentially ethically challenging situation, which in turn goes against some of the aspects of the program—the adult being an advocate with the student and developing this ongoing relationship in which they can have these in-depth, rich discussions. But the catch-22 is that if, during those discussions, the student really starts talking about serious issues, the advocate may be required by law to report it. So some of these teachers feel that they can't, by law, provide confidentiality to the students they are working with each day."

"This is a problem."

"And then on top of that, the principal, Mr. Baldwin, is trying to use the program to bring issues to the surface. But he tries to address those issues by going after personnel."

"It sounded like such a nice, simple program to help kids," said Shirah, closing her notebook. "Who would have ever thought that it would have ended up in such a mess?"

Her professor didn't say a word, but shook her head in agreement.

The following week, Professor Nephews told Shirah that she was to observe Miss Smith's advocacy group. She also advised Shirah that Miss

Smith was one of the teachers that had initially expressed concerns about the advocacy program. She said she was telling Shirah this so that she would take particular precautions to protect the teacher's confidentiality. Shirah said that she would make sure that whatever information she gathered from the setting would not be reported in any way that would specifically identify the teacher with what she said or did.

Shirah made sure to arrive early for her first observation of Miss Smith's advocacy meeting. Four students met with Miss Smith in a small room that the school used for special meetings. Three of the students were in fifth grade and one was in sixth. On the first two days of her observations Shirah noted some tension in the room. She noted that Miss Smith seemed a little reserved in how she was discussing issues with the students. For example, one student brought up the issue of making choices, particularly sorting wrong from right choices when it came to drug use, and the teacher seemed to skip over a point that could have been pursued further. Shirah thought that some of what she perceived as the teacher's holding back could have been because of *observer effect:* people who are being observed tend to act differently from how they typically act when unobserved in the same setting. Shirah had learned about observer effect in one of her research and evaluation courses, so she made a note alongside her observations that this common phenomenon might be occurring.

After a couple of observations Shirah noticed that the group seemed more relaxed. She also noted that Miss Smith did not skip over issues that students brought up as she had done before. Shirah felt as though the times she had spent in Miss Smith's advocacy group had allowed Miss Smith to develop a sense of trust in her.

Later, Shirah was in the school cafeteria getting something to eat before going on to her next observation. She felt a tap on her shoulder and turned around to find the school principal standing behind her.

He introduced himself and she did the same.

"You don't have to wait in the line with the students," he said, motioning her to follow him. "Teachers and school guests can cut to the front."

"Thank you," said Shirah. She followed him to the front of the line. "I was wondering how I would eat my lunch and get to my next appointment."

He took two of the bright orange cafeteria trays from a stack and passed one to her. "Busy with the evaluation?" he asked.

"Yes, I have some interviews to do after lunch," said Shirah. She remembered what Professor Nephews had said about the school principal, so she was on guard.

"Were you doing interviews this morning, too?"

"No, I was observing."

"Oh, that's right—I saw in the office log that you signed in to see Miss Smith."

Shirah felt herself tense up. "Yes."

"So how did her group session go?" he asked.

Shirah thought carefully about what she would say. "Good. Very good. I enjoyed it a lot."

"That's great," said the principal. "Enjoy your day." He turned to get his food and pushed his tray down the line toward the cashier.

Later, as Shirah ate her lunch, she reflected on their conversation. She thought about what the principal had asked her and how she had replied. The conversation had seemed very casual, and she was certain that she had not revealed any specific information about Miss Smith or what had gone on in the group's session that she had observed. Taking a forkful of mashed potatoes, Shirah felt relieved.

Shirah's feeling of confidence did not last for long. The next morning she returned the conference room to observe Miss Smith's advocacy group. She knocked on the door and Miss Smith answered it.

"Oh, hi," said Miss Smith. "Didn't you get my message?"

"No," said Shirah, surprised. "What message?"

"I left a message with Professor Nephews that I am uncomfortable being observed, and since it is voluntary, I would prefer not to have the evaluators sit in on our discussions."

"Oh," said Shirah. She tried to hide the disappointment in her voice. "I see. Okay then, thank you."

Miss Smith closed the door in Shirah's face.

Shirah left the school, very upset. *What did I do wrong? Why is Miss Smith suddenly so uncomfortable with having me observe the advocacy sessions? How am I going to explain this to Professor Nephews?* These questions and more raced through her mind as she drove back to the university.

Most of all, she worried whether this would compromise the entire evaluation project.

Later Shirah met with Professor Nephews to review what had happened. Apparently the principal, not meaning to, had seen Miss Smith in the hall later that day; he had told her that he'd spoken with the evaluator, who had said that the advocacy session had gone well and Miss Smith had done a good job. Miss Smith, in turn, concluded that the evaluator and principal had met purposely to discuss her work, and that if the evaluator had told him this, what else might she have told him?

Feeling that her confidentiality had been breached, Miss Smith decided that because the observations were voluntary she could choose to stop participating. This was certainly her right as a participant in the evaluation. The evaluators continued to observe advocacy session through the remainder of the school year, but no one from the evaluation team could observe Miss Smith's group again.

SUMMARY OF EVALUTION ACTIVITIES AND FINDINGS

Being an evaluator-in-training and participating in a "real" evaluation is a richly rewarding experience that can influence an evaluator for years to come. In this case study Shirah had the opportunity to both learn about program evaluation and partake in a real evaluation of an advocacy program. Despite the potential benefits of such a program, the program itself—because of the discussion sessions with students about serious issues—had some potential challenges. The most serious challenge, however, concerned confidentiality, and although Shirah went to great lengths to protect the confidentiality of her participants, in the end the teacher Shirah was observing had a different perception.

FINAL THOUGHTS

Struggling with issues surrounding confidentiality is something that every evaluator will have to deal with at some point in his or her career. Although on the surface maintaining confidentiality seems a fairly simple concept to adhere to, in reality confidentiality issues take on a completely different aspect when an evaluator steps away from the textbook definition and begins to collect data in a real-world setting.

KEY CONCEPTS

Aggregating

Debrief

DISCUSSION QUESTIONS

1. Observer effect was noted in this case study when Shirah observed students in their advocacy discussion groups. Observer effect applies

to validity of data, inasmuch as those who are being observed may not behave or respond to their setting as they usually would because of the presence of an outside observer—in this case, the program evaluator. How did Shirah deal with this possibility of observer effect? Was she successful in doing so?

2. Discuss the challenges in this case study that Shirah and her professor faced with providing confidentiality to the teachers and other staff participating as advocates in this program.

3. Some of the teachers in this program had difficulties with it because they believed it put them in an ethically compromising position. If you were a teacher in this program, how would you feel, based on what your fellow teachers in this case study would likely have shared with you?

4. Based on the outcome of the case study, if you were Shirah how would you have responded to the principal when he approached you in the lunch line that day?

CLASS ACTIVITIES

1. Unlike teachers, program evaluators are typically not considered to be *mandated reporters*. Do some research on what constitutes a mandated reporter. Interview some teachers or school administrators and find out what it means to be a mandated reporter. Find out what kind of information you must report, by law, and to whom you must report it. Then have a discussion about the possible pros and cons of being a mandated reporter. Discuss whether you think program evaluators should be considered mandated reporters and list some possible challenges if this were the case.

2. Examine the methodology used for the program evaluation. Is a possible stakeholder group (or groups) not being included in the data collection process? If so, name the group or groups and discuss how you would go about collecting data from them. Also be prepared to discuss how collecting data from the group or groups would help to strengthen the evaluation of this program.

3. Evaluations are conducted under a wide range of circumstances. The setting for this evaluation could be considered a bit hostile: the school principal's agenda for the evaluation and the evaluation

data is inherently different from that of the program evaluators. Break into small groups and, pretending that you are the evaluation team, come up with a plan for how you would continue conducting the evaluation in this setting. Think about ways in which you would report data, the type of data, and methods for data collection that would suit your plan of action. Think about ways in which you could use the aspects of evaluation just discussed to work with the principal and get him to think about the purpose of the evaluation in a different way.

SUGGESTED READING

Fitzpatrick, J. L., & Morris, M. (1999). Current and emerging ethical challenges in evaluation. *New Directions for Evaluation*, 82.

Parry, O. (2004). Whose data are they anyway? Practical, legal, and ethical issues in archiving qualitative research data. *Sociology*, *38*(1), 139–152.

Newman, D. L., & Brown, R. D. (1996). *Applied ethics for program evaluation*. State University of New York at Albany: SUNY.

CHAPTER

EVALUATION OF A SCHOOL IMPROVEMENT GRANT TO INCREASE PARENT INVOLVEMENT

LEARNING OBJECTIVES

After reading this case study you should be able to

1. Understand some of the challenges evaluators face when collecting valid interview data on site

2. Understand how an evaluator's biases may impact the data that are being collecting in a school setting

3. Recognize observer effect and be able to make recommendations for further addressing this phenomenon when collecting data

THE EVALUATORS

Matt and Linda Jackson were a husband-and-wife evaluation team. Before they became consultant evaluators they both worked for the state's education department in the division of testing and measurement. Since they became semi-retired they had worked with local school districts and not-for-profits, writing grants, providing training, and conducting program evaluation, as needed.

THE PROGRAM

Increasing parent involvement has been a challenge for many school districts throughout the country. Low parent involvement, particularly as students move from middle to junior and high school, has been well documented throughout the literature. Because of this, the state provided competitive funds or grants for school districts with low parent involvement. The monies were to be used for the district to develop a plan to increase parent involvement throughout the district. The plan had to include the establishment of at least one parent center at one of the schools. The parent center was believed to be a key element in increasing parent involvement. Under the state initiative these parent centers would also provide support for parents, parenting classes and workshops, information about other social and other support services, and so on.

Linda and Matt were hired to conduct an evaluation of ten school districts' parent involvement initiatives. Fifty schools had received monies from the parent involvement initiative grants; of these, ten districts were chosen by the state because of geographical locations across the state and other key variables (such as urban, suburban, rural).

THE EVALUATION PLAN

For their evaluation plan Linda and Matt decided to use a mixed-methods approach. To understand the breadth of parent involvement projects across all the participating districts, they prepared a two-page survey that they mailed out to the *key informant* or point person in charge of the project at each district. (In some districts these key informants are commonly referred to as *director of special projects.*) The survey was broken down into three parts. The first part would document the key components of the district's plan; for example:

- A designated area or room in the school occupied and used solely as the parent center

- A full-time or designated person to operate and direct the parent center

- Regular hours of operation (five hours a day, minimum of three days, and at least one weekend per month)

The second part of the survey would gather information from project directors about the kinds of activities and programs they had developed and implemented (training programs for parents, GED, and the like). The third part would focus on successes or outcomes they had experienced with not only increased parent involvement but also an expansion into different types of parent involvement—for example, homework help, regular attendance at school events, attendance at meetings with school staff.

In addition to this survey, the evaluators would work to gather depth of information about the program. This would include benefits and successes, as well as any challenges project directors had faced in getting these centers established and up and running in their districts. To do this the evaluators would conduct one-day site visits to the ten selected parent centers. As part of this process, they planned to conduct interviews with the building principal, parent center director, teachers and other related school staff, students, and parents. To help coordinate the event, each project director had lined up several members from each of those stakeholder groups and would assemble them throughout the day for the evaluators to interview. And to ensure that the interviews were aligned and standardized, the evaluators also developed an interview protocol to guide them when conducting their interviews.

After Linda and Matt had conducted six of the ten site visits, they took a day to go over their findings and summarize their work. At this point they were disappointed. Of the six parent centers they had visited, most were missing several of the key components required under the direction of the project. Three of the six centers did not have a permanent director at the time of the visit. Five of the six had no regular scheduled hours of operation or activities for parents to attend. And three of the six did not have a designated area for the parent center at a building in the district.

The evaluation team's seventh site visit was to Alder Central School District. Based on its rural location, they found this district demographically surprising. One-third of the students were designated *English language learners* (ELL). The school also had a large Hispanic population (about a third of the school's population) and a high transient rate (also about a third). To Linda and Matt, the demographics for the district looked more like those of a School in Need of Improvement (SINI) in a more urban area that they were used to working with, rather than a rural school district. In addition, Linda had worked with the principal of the school years before when she worked at the state's education department, and she remembered the administrator as not the most effective building leader she had ever encountered. She was not expecting to find much in the way of a successful parent center at Alder.

Pulling into the parking lot of the district's single junior high and high school building, Linda said, "I certainly hope this center is better than the ones we have seen so far this week."

"Can't be worse, can it?" said Matt.

They entered the building and headed to the office to sign in and receive their visitor badges. Putting on her badge, Linda felt a tap on her shoulder. She turned and, to her surprise, found an attractive woman with dark curly hair, a warm smile, bright eyes, and what felt like a positive aura about her.

"Hi, I'm Sophia Hernandez, the school principal." She put out her hand and shook both Linda's and Matt's. "Welcome! I am so glad that you were able to come and see what we are doing with our parent center."

"Hello," said Linda. "I was expecting Mr. Baxter. Isn't he the school principal?"

"Well," said Sophia, "you are not going to see Mr. Baxter today unless you brought along your golf clubs. He retired just after the school year started, and the district brought me in as an interim principal."

She led Linda and Matt to a large, freshly painted room with big windows and plenty of sunlight filtering in.

"This is nice," said Linda. She looked around the room, noting the new computers, the nice furniture, the racks of materials and pamphlets. She walked over and began to look through a few of the pamphlets.

"How long has the parent center been operational?" asked Matt.

"About eight months now," said an unfamiliar voice from behind them.

They all turned to see a second woman.

"Let me introduce our parent center director, Sara Benson."

Linda and Matt introduced themselves.

"Sarah is a former social worker," said Sophia. "We are very lucky to get her. She has done a wonderful job coordinating a lot of the services available to parents."

"We have an usually high migrant worker population here," said Sarah.

Linda said, "Yes, we noticed that from your district's demographics. Why is that?"

"We have a large wine industry here," said Sophia. "Migrant workers from Central America come up into the district to harvest the grapes; then they move south to pick some of the other crops."

"So one of the things I have been able to do to get parents more involved is provide a connection to some of the social services that I have contact with," said Sarah. "I recently did a session about how to get a green card. We had about eighty parents attend. Then once I get them in here, I get them hooked with what their child is doing in school and how they can help at home."

"Sounds great," said Linda.

Matt began to run down some of the question on their interview protocol. "Do you have regular hours? Workshops for parents?"

"Yes," said Sarah. She handed him a packet. "We prepared these materials for you. You'll find parent sign-in sheets for the monthly workshops we have been conducting, a schedule of hours of operation, and materials that we have handed out and used to work with parents. This month we have really been focusing on homework." She pointed to a big sign over the door that read, "Do you know where your kid is? Do you know if she has done her homework?"

"Wonderful!" said Linda.

"We have a whole agenda set up for you today," said Sophia. She handed each of them an itinerary of their interviews. "We have scheduled several parents for you to talk with at nine-thirty, then we have teachers at eleven and again at one. Then we have some students at two and some administrators at three-thirty."

"Sounds like a packed day," said Matt.

"And the nice thing is that it can all be done here in the parent center," said the principal. "I can even have lunch delivered so you don't have to go out."

"Won't you need the parent center during the day for parents?" asked Matt.

"We should be fine," said Sarah. "Wednesdays are slow at the center."

All day Linda and Matt interviewed the various stakeholders as they came in according to the schedule. It was exhausting, but by the end of the day they had spoken to everyone that they needed to.

As they left the school, Linda said, "This was, without a doubt, the best parent center we've seen."

"I agree," said Matt. "It clearly met all the program criteria."

After the long day of work Linda and Matt decided to stay in a nearby motor lodge. That evening they reviewed their notes from the day's extensive interviews. While they were working, Linda discovered that she had left part of her notes on a legal pad at the school.

The next morning, on their way out of town, Linda and Matt stopped quickly at the school to pick up the notes. They needed to get to their scheduled interviews in the next district.

Matt pulled the car up in front of the school and waited while Linda ran in.

Linda did not stop at the office to check in. Remembering where the parent center was, she made her way down the hall. When she rounded the corner to the parent center, she could hear laughter and noise coming from inside.

They must be having a parent workshop or activity, Linda thought.

She entered the parent center doorway, but did not find parents actively engaged in a workshop as she expected. Instead, she found the room full of teachers kicked back in the nice new furniture, having coffee and pastries. The new computers had been removed, as well as the rack of informational pamphlets. The bright posters and materials that had been there the day before were also gone.

The teachers stopped talking and looked at Linda. And she looked back at them, not knowing what to say or what to think.

"Can we help you?" one of the teachers finally asked.

"I came to get my notebook from yesterday," Linda replied. But she didn't know what good the notes would do now.

SUMMARY OF EVALUATION ACTIVITIES AND FINDINGS

Linda and Matt were an evaluation team with a great deal of experience in education and conducting program evaluations. In this case study the duo took on conducting site visits to ten different schools that had created parent centers to increase parent involvement. Because of their past dealings with one of the schools, the evaluators entered the setting with biases or opinions already established about the work that was going on there. Despite these biases, they were pleasantly surprised with the parent center they observed. In fact, based on their one-day site visit, they believed that the parent center could be designated a model for other schools to follow. However, this belief doesn't last long; when Linda entered the parent center unannounced the following morning, she found a scene quite different from what had been presented to them the day before.

FINAL THOUGHTS

Linda and Matt were disappointed. What they had thought was an exemplary parent center turned out to be a carefully orchestrated illusion. They completed all their site visits and submitted their evaluation report to the state. They found that all the parent centers they visited were lacking major components or criteria required of them in the grant.

Based on their evaluation data, the state decided to more closely monitor the awards given to parent centers in the future. They also decided to develop trainings to help schools more fully implement parent centers with all of the required characteristics they were looking for.

KEY CONCEPTS

Key informant

Director of special projects

English language learner

DISCUSSION QUESTIONS

1. In this case study the evaluators had the school principal arrange their interviews with the various stakeholders. Retrospectively, what are some possible disadvantages of scheduling interviews such as this? What might be some more effective ways of interfacing with stakeholder groups on site?

2. Linda was pleasantly surprised to find a new principal at the rural school. She had worked with the previous principal before in her former position at the state's education department. In addition, the demographics for the district reminded both Linda and Matt of an urban district. Considering both situations, describe how we as

evaluators bring our biases to each setting we enter. How might you, as an evaluator, try to control for some of these biases?

3. Observer effect manifests when the people you are observing act or perform in a way that is not indicative of their usual behavior. Where in this case study can you see evidence of observer effect occurring? And how could you methodologically try to correct it?

CLASS ACTIVITIES

1. See if there are any parent centers in any of the school districts in your community. As a future evaluator, set up an appointment with a school administrator to visit the parent center. See what kinds of activities these centers are offering, the type of facility, and the kinds of outcomes or changes they have seen in parent involvement as a result of implementing the center.

2. As part of their mixed methods, the evaluators conducted interviews with stakeholders. They interviewed teachers, staff, parents, and students. Develop an interview protocol that you believe could serve as a framework for the project. How would you alter items to meet the different stakeholder needs and perspectives?

SUGGESTED READING

Cooper, C. W., & Christie, C. A. (2005). Evaluating parent empowerment: A look at the potential of social justice evaluation in education. *Teacher College Record, 107*(10), 2248–2274.

Reutzel, R. D., Fawson, P.C., & Smith J. A. (2006). Words to go: Evaluating a first-grade parent involvement program for making words at home. *Reading Research and Instruction, 45*(20), 119–159.

REFERENCES

Barton, J., & Collins, A. (1997). *Portfolio assessment: A handbook for educators.* Menlo Park, CA: Addison-Wesley.

Brown, R. D. (1985). Supervising evaluation practicum and intern students: A developmental model. *Educational Evaluation and Policy Analysis, 7*(2), 161–167.

Chelimsky, E. (1997). The political environment of evaluation and what it means for the development of the field. In E. Chelimsky & W. Shadish (eds.), *Evaluation for the 21st century* (pp. 53–68). Thousand Oaks, CA: Sage.

Elmore, R. F. (1993). *The development and implementation of large-scale curriculum reforms.* Cambridge, MA: Harvard Graduate School of Education, Center for Policy Research in Education.

Elmore, R. F. (1996). Getting to scale with good educational practice. *Harvard Educational Review, 66*(1), 1–25.

Fitzpatrick, J. B., Sanders, B. L., & Worthen, J. F. (2004). *Program evaluation: Alternative approaches and practical guidelines.* Boston: Allyn & Bacon.

Klecker, B. (2000, March). Content validity of pre-service teacher portfolios in a standards-based program. *Journal of Instructional Psychology, 27*(1), 35–38.

Lodico, M. G., Spaulding, D. T., & Voegtle, K. H. (2006). *Methods in educational research: From theory to practice.* San Francisco: Jossey-Bass.

Mathison, S. (2005). *Encyclopedia of evaluation.* Thousand Oaks, CA: Sage.

Morgan, B. M. (1999). Portfolios in a pre-service teacher field-based program: Evolution of a rubric for performance assessment. *Education, 119*(3), 416–26.

Patton, M. Q. (1997). *Utilization-focused evaluation: The new century text.* (ERIC Document Reproduction Service NO. ED 413 355). Retrieved July 7, 2005, from ERIC database.

Patton, M. Q., & Patrizi, P. (Spring 2005). Teaching evaluation using the case method. *New Directions for Evaluation*, 105. San Francisco: Jossey-Bass.

Piaget, J., and Imhelder, B. (1969). *The psychology of the child.* New York: Basic Books.

Rogers, P. J. (2005). Logic Models. In S. Mathison (Ed.), *Encyclopedia of evaluation* (pp. 232–235). Thousand Oaks, CA: Sage.

Roth, W. M. (1994). Experimenting in a constructivist high school physics laboratory. *Journal of Research in Science Teaching, 1*(2), 197–223.

Shannon, D. M., & Boll, M. (1996). Assessment of preservice teachers using alternative assessment methods. *Journal of Personnel Evaluation in Education, 10*(2), 117–35.

Spaulding, D. T., & Lodico, M. G. (2003). *Providing hands-on learning opportunities for evaluators-in-training: A model for classroom desig*n. Paper presented at the Annual American Evaluation Association Conference, Reno, NV.

Spaulding, D. T., & Straut, D. (2006, March). *Using e-portfolios to document teacher candidate experiences with technology integration during field placements: A validation study.* Paper presented at the Society for Information Technology and Teacher Education (SITE) Annual Conference, Orlando, FL.

Spaulding, D. T., Straut, D., Wright, T., & Cakar, D. (2005, April). *The fundamentals of validation: A three-phase plan for year-one evaluation of a PT3 Project to transform teacher education through the use of technology.* Paper presented at the Society for Information Technology and Teacher Education (SITE) Annual Conference, Phoenix, AZ.

Trevisan, M. S. (2002). Enhancing practical evaluation training through long-term evaluation projects. *American Journal of Evaluation, 23*(1), 81–92.

Weeks, E. C. (1982). The value of experiential approaches to evaluation training. *Evaluation and Program Planning, 5,* 21–30.

Wiggins, G. (1992). Creative test worth taking. *Educational Leadership, 49*(8), 26–34.

Wiggins, G. (1998). *Educative assessment: Designing assessment to inform and improve student performance.* San Francisco: Jossey-Bass.

INDEX